RUSSIA AND JAPAN

MAURICE HINDUS

RUSSIA
AND
JAPAN

DOUBLEDAY, DORAN AND COMPANY, INC.
Garden City 1942 *New York*

327.47
H588

Acknowledgment

PARTS OF CERTAIN CHAPTERS have appeared in the
Toronto *Star Weekly,* and to the editor of this
publication I wish to express thanks for permission to use the material in this book. I am also
indebted to the American-Russian Institute for
permission to reproduce some of their up-to-date
maps.

MAURICE HINDUS.

Contents

The Great Test in Europe

CHAPTER I

The Irrepressible Conflict

A WAR between Russia and Japan is as inevitable as was the war between Russia and Germany. Only the sudden collapse of Japan would avert such a war. Triumph in the southern Pacific must only hasten it. The long-standing differences between the two nations, in the words of Sir Stafford Cripps, "can never be settled except by force."

Just as Germany never could hope to realize her far-flung world aims without conquering Russia, so Japan, the Prussia of Asia as she is often called, can have no hope of achieving her world aims or even her ambitions in Asia without pushing Russia out of her way with all the violence that she can muster.

The outside world, with only a few notable exceptions, had deemed the German-Russian non-aggression pact of August 23, 1939, a possible prelude not to a war between the two countries, but to a partnership which might result in a military alliance; it did so because it appraised the event in terms of outward appearances and immediate consequences rather than in terms of Hitler's long-range purposes and of Russia's equally long-range aim to frustrate these purposes. Only those who knew and steadily kept in mind the irreconcilable nature of the two hostile aims could foresee that an armed conflict between the two was as irrepressible as the flow of water over a shattered dam.

The same holds true of Japan. The Neutrality Pact which Matsuoko negotiated with Moscow in April 1941 was the Far Eastern equivalent of the Russo-German Pact. On both sides the motions were the same—hot enmity prior to the time of the consummation of the agreement, loudly proclaimed amity afterwards, but no change, not a hint of it, in the fundamental antagonisms of the two nations. Therefore, as in the case of Germany, the consequences are destined to be the same. Like Germany, Japan made the pact for the sake of a temporary advantage to promote a long-range purpose, which Russia must of necessity frustrate with her blood in order to survive in Asia or indeed at all.

The basic facts and issues of the irrepressible conflict between Japan and Russia are clear once we are ready to face them. Nor is this conflict any longer in the future tense. Russia and Japan have been unofficially and almost uninterruptedly at war for nearly a decade. The governments of the two countries have exchanged countless notes of sharpest protest and indignation. Japanese and Soviet publications have engaged in protracted and bitter duels of words. In Japan there has grown up a monumental literature on the nature of the quarrels with Russia and of the war that must be fought with the Soviets. Less imposing is the literature on the same subject that the Soviets have in recent years accumulated.

One of the most vivid literary contributions to the subject is a novel entitled *Red Planes Fly East,* by Piotr Pavlenko, one of the better-known Russian writers. Suggestive and significant are the chapter headings. The first begins with May 1932 and is worded: "One Plane Flew from Moscow to the East," and by the time the story reaches December 1934 the title of the chapter reads: "In Weather Which Registered Fifty Degrees Below Zero, Four Hundred Aeroplanes Flew to the East." The month in which the war starts is March. In this novel the Soviets lost battles but won the war.

The difference in the content of the two literatures on the forthcoming war is striking: the Japanese not only discuss the cause of the quarrels, but the nature of their ambitions, also the military methods of settling and ending the quarrels and of attaining their ambitions. The Russians, except in the aforementioned novel, center their rhetorical fire on Japan's threats of war, with hardly a word as to their methods of fighting it and with emphasis on their desire to avoid it but not at the sacrifice of their own sovereignty.

Most significant of all—the troops of both lands have clashed in combat all along the far-stretching borders of

Manchukuo and Siberia. Up to date, at a conservative estimate, the two opposing armies have fought no less than
twenty-five hundred border skirmishes that now and then
attained the magnitude and ferocity of large-scale battles in
which all weapons of modern warfare, from rifle to bayonet,
from tank to airplane, were employed.

As in the case of the Russo-German conflict, the aggressor has been the Fascist power. The difference is that the
German invasion in the summer of 1941 was the final test
of arms, while the Japanese assaults over the past decade
have been preliminary tests, with a view to taking the
measure of the Red armies in all departments of warfare
so as to appraise their strength and develop effective ways
of overcoming it. But the decisive test of arms is bound to
come perhaps sooner than we imagine, while Japan is victorious on the fronts on which she is already waging war,
just as the final test of arms with Germany had to come
when the Nazi armies remained unvanquished in the
battlefields of the west.

As in the case of Germany, and with a frankness which
is so fantastic that the outside world has ignored it, Japanese spokesmen have repeatedly been announcing this
coming conflict with Russia.

Consider the utterance of the League of State Construction, a definitely Fascist Japanese organization, made on
October 10, 1933, in an appeal to the Japanese Minister of
Foreign Affairs: "Red Russia is the direct enemy of Japan;
unless she is destroyed there is no prospect for the Empire

but disintegration."[1] Japanese writings and speeches on Russia bristle with similar sentiments.

But again, as in the instance of the Nazis, Russia has taken Japanese rhetorical defiance earnestly to heart and has countered swiftly and firmly the threats and the assaults.

In subsequent chapters I shall present in detail the multitude of irreconcilable conflicts between Russia and Japan—economic, political, geographic, social, ideological —irreconcilable only because to attain her imperialist ends Japan must paralyze Russia's development and influence in Asia. Japan's military and diplomatic strategy so closely parallels Hitler's that one is inclined to believe the two, despite implacable self-interest, have agreed on common methods of procedure in the global war they are waging and must continue to wage to win the ends they are jointly and separately seeking.

In the prewar days Hitler singled out Russia as his and mankind's enemy number one. So did Japan, though she never had failed to register an animosity almost as bitter toward the United States. Openly and clamorously Hitler vowed to annihilate Russia. So did Japan in the voice of leading generals and statesmen, though not always with as profligate a brashness as did Hitler. In November 1938 General Tojo, now the Premier of Japan, then vice-Minister of War, in arguing for an increased military budget, announced to the Diet that the country must be ready for "simultaneous action on two fronts—against the U.S.S.R.

[1] *When Japan Goes to War,* by E. Iogan and O. Tanin.

and against China." These words have reverberated from one end of Russia to the other. In 1939–40 General Itagaki, Japanese Minister of War appearing before the Diet on a mission similar to that of General Tojo, again pointed to Russia as one of the reasons for the mounting military expenditures. Since neither General Tojo nor General Itagaki would at that time consider the long-standing Russian offer for a non-aggression pact, which on paper at least would commit both nations to a policy of peace, the allusion to "simultaneous action on two fronts" can have only one meaning, especially to the Russians—a planned offensive against them.

As time for war drew near it was with Russia, the enemy to be annihilated, that Hitler concluded a non-aggression pact. So did Japan, though she had to content herself only with a neutrality agreement. Hitler signed the pact to avoid fighting simultaneously on two widely separated fronts. This is precisely the reason Japan has followed in his footsteps. Hitler sought to win the battle of the seas—primarily against the British navy—before launching his crusade against Russia's land army. Japan too has sought to win the battle of the seas—primarily against the American navy—before launching an all-out attack on the Russian land armies. Just as Hitler did not want to fight the British navy and the Russian army at the same time, so Japan did not want to fight the American navy and the Russian army at the same time. When Hitler concluded the non-aggression pact with Russia he had not the least intention to abide by it. Neither has Japan any wish to abide by her neutrality agreements, otherwise the Japanese press would cease to harangue Russia and to boast of coming conquests of Russian lands. Japan's record in the breaking of treaties is no less spectacular than is that of Germany.

This similarity of policy between Japan and Nazi Germany can hardly be an accident. Nor is it an accident that on December 8, the day after Japan's attack on Pearl Harbor, Hitler officially called off the offensive against Moscow. In the light of these two events Hitler's quarrel with his generals and the purely artificial aspect of the German-Japanese alliance, however much the two may now co-operate, assume a fresher and clearer meaning.

Obviously Hitler was faced with one of two choices. He could follow the advice of his generals and cease the offensive on Moscow long before the actual arrival of the Russian winter—thereby perhaps forfeiting the advantage of an immediate Japanese attack on his enemies— or he could press on with the offensive, driving at all costs closer and closer to Moscow, with a view to convincing Japan of Russia's military helplessness in Europe and thus inveigle her into immediate action against the American navy. We now know the choice Hitler made.

The endless and boastful communiqués of the German High Command and of other Nazi propaganda agencies, announcing "stupendous," "momentous," "unheard-of," "unparalleled," "spectacular" victories on the Russian front and Hitler's ringing proclamations that the Red armies were at his feet gasping for breath, were intended not only to pamper Nazi vanity and to reassure the German people of an impending end to their sacrifices, but to overcome possible hesitation of the Japanese militarists to strike at America.

The question naturally arises: would Japan have made the spectacular plunge into war on December 7 had she known or suspected that the very next day the German High Command would announce that the war in Russia "will now be dictated by winter," and that the German armies would be "digging in" all along the far-flung front? The very haste with which Hitler acted on the Russian front, once Japan was embroiled in combat with America and with the other sea powers of the Pacific, rouses endless speculation.

But now that Japan is in the war and knows only too clearly that Russia is a formidable power she must go on, regardless of consequences. More than ever must Japan be prepared to fight Russia, for if the Soviets win against Hitler they become more than ever a menace to Japan's fondest ambitions. Besides, never again may Japan have the chance to fight Russia while the Red armies must contend with the formidable Reichswehr on another front, thousands of miles away from the Far East.

As for Russia, if only because of the physical exhaustion that followed the civil war, and later because of the aim quickly to industrialize herself, she has been pursuing a policy of peace, but not of peace at any price. This policy may best be expressed in Theodore Roosevelt's historic words: "Speak softly and carry a big stick." Most of the outside world suspected the sincerity of these words or treated them with contempt. It pointed to the presence of Communist parties in other countries and to the class war they were championing as the reason for the hostile attitude. It didn't seriously consider Moscow's peace proposals, not even when, in violation of his spoken word and his written pledge, Hitler occupied Czechoslovakia.

Still less did the outside world have faith in the reality and the power of Russia's "big stick." To the physical eye it looked neither big nor strong. To many, indeed to the overwhelming majority of foreign observers, diplomats, and military attachés in Moscow—including, of course, the Germans—the stick appeared no more than a shriveled twig which a violent gust of wind would blow away. They said so publicly and privately, in official dispatches and at dinner tables.

But Russia went on with the policy of the "soft speech" and the "big stick." She sought peace but prepared for war. Her methods were in gross violation of established economic usage and of traditional social morality. Violently she proceeded to supplant private enterprise with state collectivized effort and to intensify the propagation and enforcement of her own morality and her own ideology. To the Kremlin, the combination of the Soviet idea of collectivized instead of private ownership and the modern machine was destined to achieve miracles in the rapid industrialization of the country and once for all solve Russia's pressing problems of peace and war. No-where else, at no other time in history, had so grandiose

an undertaking been attempted and on so gigantic a scale.
It defied the reality, the habit, the credibility of a world
that has been nurtured in political democracy and made
rich and powerful under a system of private enterprise.
That was why it roused doubt in the reality and the power
of the Soviet method and the Soviet "big stick," which
the Five-Year Plans had commenced in earnest to forge.
Hence also the puzzle of Soviet internal policy with its
endless shift of emphasis from new to old usage and from
old to new again. Annually, because of the strange new
measures the Soviet was forcibly inaugurating, the puzzle
grew more and more inexplicable, more and more exasperating to the perennial foe no less than to the once-
fervent friend.

But the work went on, regardless of cost and with no
concession to foreign doubt and foreign denunciation. Increasingly Moscow centered its energy on the "big stick,"
on which it had set its heart and mind and on which it
had staked its future. No opposition was entertained or
tolerated, was indeed cruelly and summarily suppressed,
which only further intensified the puzzle and the exaspera-
tion as well as the disbelief in the ultimate achievement.

Illuminating today is Stalin's discussion in 1934 of the
coming conflict with Germany and Japan. Both countries
had already withdrawn from the League of Nations and
were pursuing provocative policies toward Russia and
other neighbors.

"Again as in 1914," said Stalin, "the parties of bellicose
imperialism, the parties of war and *revanche* are coming

into the foreground. Quite clearly things are moving toward a new war."

Then speaking of the possible war makers, with clear implications of the impending Russo-German clash, he goes on: "Still others think that war should be organized by a 'superior race,' say the German 'race' against an 'inferior race,' *primarily against the Slavs* [author's italics], that only such a war can provide a way out of the situation because it is the mission of the 'superior race' to fertilize the 'inferior race' and to rule over it.

"Let us assume that this queer theory, which is as far removed from science as heaven is from earth, is put into practice. What will come of it? It is well known that ancient Rome regarded the ancestors of the present-day Germans and French in the same way in which the representatives of the 'superior race' now regard the Slavonic tribes. It is well known that ancient Rome treated them as an 'inferior race,' as 'barbarians' whose destiny it was to be eternally subordinated to the 'superior race,' to 'Great Rome,' and between ourselves let it be said that ancient Rome had some grounds for this, which cannot be said about the representatives of the present 'superior race.' But what came of it? The result was that non-Romans, that is, all the 'barbarians' united against the common enemy, hurled themselves against Rome and overthrew it.

"The question arises: What guarantee is there that the claims of the representatives of the present 'superior race' will not lead to deplorable results? What guarantee is there that the Fascist literary politicians in Berlin will be more fortunate than the ancient and experienced conquerors of Rome? Would it not be more correct to say that the opposite will be the case?"

Then turning to the brewing conflicts between Russia and Japan, Stalin says:

"One section of the military men in Japan are openly advocating in the press the necessity of a war against the U.S.S.R. and the seizure of the Maritime Provinces with the avowed approval of another section of the military, while the Government of Japan, instead of calling these instigators of war to order, is pretending that it is a matter of no concern to itself. It is not difficult to understand that such circumstances cannot but create an atmosphere of uneasiness and uncertainty."

Further expounding Russia's policy of "speak softly and carry a big stick," Stalin continues:

"Of course we shall continue persistently to pursue the policy of peace and strive for an improvement in our relations with Japan because we want to improve these relations. But it does not entirely depend on us. That is why we must at the same time adopt all measures for the purpose of guarding our country against surprises and be prepared to defend it in the event of attack."

Stalin ends the discussion of the threatened attacks by Germany and Japan with words that immediately became national slogans:

"Those who want peace and are striving for business intercourse with us will receive our support. Those who seek to attack our country will receive a stunning rebuff and will be taught never again to poke their pig's snout into our garden patch."

From these words it is clear that in 1934 Stalin was under no illusion as to the possibility of official friendship with Germany and Japan. The spirit of tough defiance in the last sentence I have quoted speaks for itself. Stalin hoped for the best, but was preparing for the worst—for war against Germany and Japan at the same time and without allies. The Anti-Comintern Pact which Japan and Germany signed on November 25, 1936, spelled to the Russians—leaders and people—only one thing: a military alliance against them. The loudness with which the pact was proclaimed only accentuated this conviction. "Today I am plowing for spring wheat," said a young peasant to me on a collective farm outside of Moscow. "Tomorrow or the day after I may have to snipe at Japanese or Germans. I am a good marksman. I'll make a good guerrilla."

Widespread over Russia was this belief at the time. Yet now, however heavy Russia's ordeal, it is infinitely more light than Russia had imagined it would be. China, England, the United States are her fighting allies! Such good fortune, indeed such an historic miracle, neither leaders nor people had anticipated. But neither had they anticipated Munich in all its far-reaching consequences, particularly the formidable industrial, military, labor power, which it would enable Nazi Germany quickly to amass and to exploit for purposes of conquest. Still less did they anticipate the swift collapse of France and the benefits, especially military, that this would make possible for Hitler.

The war with Germany has revealed a Russia that to the outside world was not supposed to exist, something too incredible to be true. "If Russia can be kept in the war until winter," said the New York *Times* in an editorial on June 24, "it may make all the difference in the world." It is well enough for the atrocity school of American writers on Russia to continue picturing Russia as a land of cruelty and gore and nothing else. Yet the fighting on the Russian front goes on, and because of that alone, and even if the Red armies are again overcome by reverses, Russia is one of the overwhelming and decisive factors of our time.

On the outbreak of the Russo-German war I wrote *Hitler Cannot Conquer Russia,* not as a prediction but as an exposition. I attempted to give a picture of a Russia which, despite external symbols and appearances, abounded in powers that were not as open to the physical eye as in an established country, and that would make it impossible for Hitler to defeat her. "He may sweep over the Ukraine," I wrote, "up central and northern Russia. He may seize Kiev, Kharkov, Rostov, Leningrad, and Moscow. He may push eastward to the Urals. But he will not win the war, because he cannot hold the Russian earth and Russian humanity."

Now that the war with Japan—which the Russians had for years been expecting, which the Japanese have freely been threatening and yearning to make—have in fact attempted to wage—is becoming more and more of a certainty, it is all the more urgent to make an appraisal of the powers of Russia which make her, in this writer's judgment, unconquerable. I firmly believe that even a combination of the Japanese and the German armies cannot vanquish the Russian people. Space alone, always one of Russia's stanchest allies, will prevent that. Foreign armies may wrest enormous territories from Russia, kill millions of soldiers and civilians, lay waste many Russian lands. Japan may drive Soviet armies to Lake Baikal or even west of this focal dividing line in. Siberia. Germany may oust the Soviets from. European Russia. This is the very worst that can happen, though now the very thought of it seems absurd. But the fighting will not stop. There will still be a front over an enormous territory. There will still be guerillas in the midst and in the rear of the enemy. There will be ruin and desolation, but there will be a fighting spirit and fighting weapons for millions of men and women. Not even the signing of a separate peace with a Moscow government, were it ever to come, would kill this spirit or destroy these weapons. The forces of Russian history, Russian geography, above all the forces of the Revolution, would make this impossible.

More and more the world will look back to the year 1928, the year of the first Five-Year Plan, as the great turning point in Russian history. It is the three Five-Year Plans which Russia has barely completed that have given the country the strength it never has had. More than ever is it true, as the late General von Hindenburg said, that "Russia has no heart at which to strike." Because of what has happened in Siberia alone, Russia can move her "heart" to regions beyond the reach of the most powerful gun and the most skilled gunner.

The edict which the Moscow Government has recently issued, banning the return home of the refugees who have fled in advance of the German armies, is full of meaning. It signifies that Russia is resolved to fortify herself with fresh millions in her Asiatic lands, which in itself must stir the wrath and the fighting ardor of the Japanese generals, who long ago had included at least eastern Siberia in their *Lebensraum* and in their scheme of "Asia for the Asiatics." Because of Russian geography—particularly because of what has been happening in Siberia, this great wonderland of Russia—millions and millions of men and women can withdraw into vast steppes and forests, raise food, manufacture armaments, from bayonets to tanks and bombers, and keep on with the war. Neither the Germans nor the Japanese, with all the troubles they will have in the Russian lands they may occupy, can ever muster armies large enough to penetrate these steppes and forests and strike the fatal blow.

It is well, therefore, to appraise anew the powers at the command of the Russian people in this war of life and death not only of a nation but of an idea. That is why I have divided this book into two parts. The first four chapters give a picture at one time puzzling and mysterious, now in retrospect clear and meaningful, by which the Soviet Union has marshaled its resources and people into the "big stick" it has been wielding against the Reichswehr. The more we know of the nature and sources of Russia's fighting spirit in Europe and the methods by which these have been built up and exploited, the better we can evaluate the achievements of the Russian armies after nine months of fighting, and the more fully prepared will we be to appraise Russia's position in the Far East. To Russia more even than to America, if only because of the war she is now fighting with Germany, the events in Europe are inextricably linked to those of Asia. Indeed, the war in Europe must only hasten the showdown in Asia. Nothing Hitler needs more than a diversion for the Russian armies in the Far East, and nothing, as will be shown later, is so opportune for Japan as to fight Russia while her main armies are at war in Europe.

The remaining and by far the larger part of the book narrates in detail the long-standing and irrepressible conflict between Russia and the Far Eastern end of the Axis and the war the two must fight unless Japan suffers sudden collapse.

CHAPTER II

The Power of the Idea

THE RUSSIAN WINTER offensive of 1942 may come to a halt. The Red armies may again, as in the first five months of fighting, be face to face with stern reverses. Neither Russian generals nor political leaders, while supremely confident of ultimate victory, fail to warn their people of such a possibility. After the fall of Mozhaisk, Hitler's mighty outpost in his thrust on Moscow, and of Kholm, only slightly less mighty an outpost in his thrust on Leningrad, General Govrov reminded the jubilant Russian masses that "the German army is still unquestionably very powerful, and under no circumstances must we say it has been routed. It is certain the Germans will resume mass attack next spring in order to take advantage of their superiority in tanks." On February 23, 1942, on the occasion of the twenty-third anniversary of the Red army, Stalin reaffirmed this warning. "The enemy," he said, "faces defeat, but he is not yet defeated. The enemy is still strong and will exercise his last strength in order to achieve success. The more defeat threatens him, the more bestial he will become."

Nor have the Germans been reticent on their forthcoming war of revenge against Russia. In his speech of January 30, 1942, on the occasion of the ninth anniversary of his rise to power, Hitler, while insisting that he was fighting not Russians but the Russian winter, promised a savage reckoning with the Red armies. His own armies, he said, "have now become victims of frost," but spring was in the offing and they would triumph again. Hitler has every motive in the world to avenge the reverses he has suffered in Russia.

Yet at the present writing, after nine months of war, what a change in Russia, what a change in Germany, above all what a change in the world's estimate and esteem of Russia's fighting forces! The galaxy of radio commentators, professional Sovietophobes, generals, diplomats, military experts, who had foretold the collapse and destruction of the Russian armies within three or six weeks, are eloquently silent on their dire predictions. No one now wants to remember that on the outbreak of the Russo-German war they had said, or had heard others say, that the German army would cut through Russia "like a knife through butter."

The gloom that is now emanating from the Russian battlefield is not of Russian but of German origin. The Führer continues to thunder abuse and anathemas at the Russian people. But where his 1941 New Year's message had promised "the consummation of the greatest victory in history" within the year, his New Year's pronouncement of 1942 neither contains nor conveys such a happy augury. With a show of unexpected restraint, he allows himself to say only, "We can ask of the Almighty to give the German people and the German soldiers strength to resist with valiant hearts for the maintenance of our liberties and our future." To resist, not to conquer—strange language for the commander in chief of the armies of "the race of overlords!"

Nor does his speech of January 30, 1942, despite the boast of eventual victory, specify the time of its occurrence. "I do not know whether the war will end in 1942, but this I do know, let the opponent appear anywhere and we shall beat him as we have always beaten him."

Assurance, promise, hope, boast—but no more from the Führer himself! Epochal is this reversal of rhetoric and sentiment.

Today, while the Russians are holding the initiative, it is not the German radio and German propaganda that scream at Russian soldiers "surrender or die," as they had once screamed, with supreme audacity and self-confidence, at the British people. It is the Russian radio and the Russian propaganda, as at Mozhaisk, at Staraia Russa, at Orel, at Klin, that thundered this awesome message at German soldiers. In the light of Hitler's successes in the conquered countries and in the first five months of fighting in Russia, and in spite of possible future successes, it seems like a miracle that anyone, least of all "swinish" and "inferior" Russians, should hurl such defiance at Nazi armies.

Nazi after Nazi—general, politician, writer, editor—no longer wants to be reminded of the German announcement earlier in the war, that Russian resistance "is already broken and will never rise again," or of the Führer's boast of October 2, 1941, that "the Russian armies are now in the process of being annihilated," and of the radio announcement of November 8, 1941, "that the Soviet empire is smashed. No army can recover from such losses." Impatient and desperate for victory, Hitler felt constrained to say that "the enemy is fighting with a bestial lust," which, translated into sober words, means that the Russian soldiers are killing more Germans than he or his High Command had ever imagined they could!

Nazi spokesmen are confessing to the German people that they had grossly underestimated the fighting qualities of the Russian soldier. Colonel Georg Soldan, writing in Hitler's own *Völkischer Beobachter,* said that Russia is showing "an almost unimaginable power of resistance on all fronts." He is bewildered by "the toughness and staying power of the Soviet soldier." In World War I, he complains, the Russian soldier was decidedly inferior to the German, but now the Russian soldier is "hardly inferior to the German." This is extraordinary language coming from so high a Nazi source and printed in the Führer's personal newspaper—the very organ which since the day it was founded has vaunted and glorified the matchless supremacy of Germans in all avenues of human endeavor, particularly in the art and science of military combat.

Dr. Otto Dietrich, the Führer's personal press chief, informed the German people, in a special article that was printed in all German newspapers, that the misfortunes of the German armies in Russia have become serious, or, as he phrases it, "have entered an extremely serious, indeed a critical phase."

Germans now speak not of a Siegfried Line made of concrete to halt the advancing Russians, but of "a wall of blood," German blood, which, according to Hitler's original promises, repeated over and over with ever-heightening emotion in the first six years of his dictatorship, would never be shed on the battlefield. "I'm not crazy enough to want war . . . I want a monument in the hearts of my people. A thirty-centimeter shell costs two thousand marks. If I have another thousand marks I can build a workman's home." How ancient and puerile these words now sound!

Illuminating is the correspondence from the front by the editor of the *Koelnische Zeitung,* one of the most influential journals in old Germany and still commanding a widespread hearing. In one of his long dispatches this editor offers hardly a cheering word to his readers. His picture of the plight of the German soldier is the grimmest any German writer has allowed himself to portray. The German soldiers, he laments, "were never safe from attack . . . there was no time to sleep or to eat." Especially significant is his mention of the village of Borodino. Indeed, the only words of consolation he permits himself is the boast of the matchless successes of the German armies before reaching this historic village.

Let it be noted that it was at Borodino, in 1812, that Kutuzov, the Russian commander in chief, had resolved to test the fighting powers of Napoleon's Grande Armée. Napoleon was only too happy to accept the challenge. In his pursuit of the Russian armies after leaving Smolensk, he had vainly sought to catch up with them and to engage them in battle. Now his chance came. He had been invincible for fifteen years. Army after army had collapsed at the mere advent of his own forces. If Kutuzov's armies were annihilated, Russia would be at his feet, and he would be in complete mastery of the European continent.

The battle of Borodino was fought with fierceness on both sides. Napoleon won the victory, but instead of annihilating Kutuzov he only made the cunning Russian take to his heels again. According to Russian historians, it was at Borodino that Napoleon really lost the Russian war. He had won the battle, but never before had he suffered such heavy casualties. The subsequent occupation of Moscow, empty not only of Kutuzov and his armies but of most of the civilian population, did not banish Napoleon's uneasiness over the French catastrophe at Borodino. He felt troubled and shaken; he never recovered from the blow.

Doubtless it is because of present German reverses in Russia that the mention of Napoleon's name in connection with the German campaign has been forbidden in Germany. Yet the German editor's boast of German successes all the way to the gateway of Borodino has an ominous sound. Why mention this village by name when the German offensive had carried the German armies beyond it and much closer to Moscow?

Most noteworthy is the comment of an Italian correspondent on the Russian front. In their reports of the Russo-German war the Italians have been more candid than the Germans and at times have betrayed disillusionment and contrition. Early in January the correspondent of *Corriera della Sera* of Milan wrote, "The German soldier is no longer the natty, jaunty young fellow who went out to battle for his country. His uniform is dirty, his boots are run over, he needs a shave . . . but he has not time to look out for his personal appearance at the front." When the German falls back from the front lines, away from the scene of immediate fighting, "his mien is somber and he says nothing. He is a much different soldier from that of the campaigns of 1939 and 1940."

The description reads almost like Tolstoy's account in *War and Peace* of the retreating French soldiers in 1812. It has the same ring of blasted hope and mutilated pride.

Equally enlightening is the Italian writer's explanation of the cause of the breath-taking change. Referring to the harshness of the Russian earth, he speaks of "the frozen wastes, the marshes, the villages reduced to ashes, the death which pervades." The German soldier had not counted on such cruelty in nature. No one had prepared him for the inhospitable mood of the Russian earth, nor for the fighting madness of Russian humanity. "The type of fighting," the Italian continues, "the ferocity with which the Soviet soldier fights, the indifference with which he dies, his mortal hate and war without quarter, the sabotage, the constant and spine-tickling danger of mines, the interminable massacre—yes, all that and more has contributed to the slough of indifference and to the bitterness written on the faces of the Wehrmacht." Maybe it is because the Russian earth has always been hostile to an invader that the Russians speak of it as their "little mother earth" and have endowed it in song and legend with the virtues and the mercifulness of a mother.

Yet there was a time when Hitler himself had appreciated only too clearly, almost poignantly, the power of murderous revenge in the Russian earth. Its vastness had overawed him and he had not even hinted of a method of overcoming it. Writing in *Mein Kampf* of the German fighting in Russia in 1918, he says: "The greater the amount of room a people has at its disposal, the greater also is its natural protection. . . . The size of the territory gives protection against frivolous attacks. . . . And therefore the risk of an important attack, except for quite unusual reasons, will appear too great." Reading these words now it seems as though Hitler was foretelling his own failure on the Russian battlefield.

More explicit is Oswald Spengler's judgment of the Russian earth and of the powers of doom its vastness alone holds for an invader. This gloomy philosopher who foreshadowed so many of Hitler's impassioned hates, in speaking in *The Hour of Decision* of Russia, which he despised no less venomously than Hitler himself, said: "Distance is a *force,* politically and militarily, which has not yet been conquered. What good does it do the enemy to occupy areas no matter how immense? To make even the attempt impossible the Bolsheviks have transferred the center of gravity of their system farther and farther eastward." To Spengler, more than crushing is the fact that "the whole area west of Moscow—White Russia, the Ukraine, once from Riga to Odessa the most vital portion of the Czar's empire—forms today a fantastic glacis against 'Europe.' *It could be sacrificed without a crash of the whole system. But by the same token any idea of an offensive from the west has become senseless. It would be a thrust into empty space."* [Author's italics.]

Spengler's prophecies and forebodings hold out neither comfort nor hope to Hitler and the German people. Grimly and clearly he tells them that even if an invader succeeds in occupying all of European Russia, he has not won his battle, because Russia's vastness makes her lands unconquerable.

Thus, after nine months of fighting, the Russian earth and Russian humanity have remained unconquered. The big test is yet to come, indeed, the biggest, when Japan joins Germany in the battle of Russia. But with America in the war, the ordeal of the Russian armies will be lightened.

In the leading editorial of December 21, 1941, summing

up the results of the Russo-German war after six months of fighting, the New York *Times* makes this extraordinary admission: "Let us recall what the situation was in the few weeks before the invasion began. *That Hitler would attack Russia seemed hardly credible.* [Author's italics.] The possibility that was taken much more seriously in England and America and in all neutral countries was that there would be an outright military alliance between Hitler and Stalin instead of the 'economic collaboration' that had previously existed. How terribly formidable that military alliance would have been the world now knows. But last June the strength of Russia as compared with Germany was nearly everywhere underestimated. In retrospect one would almost be tempted to think that Stalin had deliberately staged his very inefficient war against Finland in order to lure Hitler on."

In retrospect one would not "almost be tempted to think," but one would be obliged to say that the hate of the Revolution, of the Soviets, of Stalin, and of Russian foreign diplomacy, especially since August 1939, had paralyzed even the desire in the outside world to see in Soviet Russia anything but a land of atrocities or a cesspool of weakness and wickedness. Overwhelming at every hand in the writings as well as in the practices of Nazi Germany and Soviet Russia was the evidence that, though both were ruthless dictatorships—which Americans would abhor and would never tolerate—not only Hitler and Stalin, but Nazism and Sovietism, were mortal enemies, with a clash in ideology, aim, ambition, everyday pursuit, which sooner or later would precipitate the fight unto death which Hitler had launched on June 22, 1941. But at that time it was easier to say and to believe the opposite, particularly for people accustomed to the full enjoyment of civil liberties and with an utter abhorrence of Sovietism and all that it implied. Therefore, Russia's war on Finland and the absorption of the Baltic states, of eastern Poland, of Bessarabia, of Galicia, loomed not at all as a preparation for a war with Germany, but as acts of wanton imperialist aggression. The terror of the Russian Revolution, its demolition of private enterprise in Russia and Soviet appeasement of Nazi Germany since August 23, 1939, though never at the expense of sovereignty, had, as it were, goaded the outside world into an acceptance of Sovietism, now more than ever, as an agency pre-eminently of destructiveness, with little or no creativeness in spirit, in idea, in achievement.

This, of course, has been the fate of all revolutionary movements, not excluding the American. Their aims are usually in such complete violation of existing modes of thought, their methods are in such brutal disregard of prevailing standards of individual and social behavior, that invariably they invoke the contempt and the wrath of contemporaries, of their immediate enemies, and of people and countries that enjoy a normal and, to themselves, a hallowed and contented way of life. In his highly readable novel, *Oliver Wiswell,* Kenneth Roberts paints on a gigantic scale this very aspect of the American Revolution. The genial, cultivated, and polished Oliver, with firm faith in

Tory righteousness and Tory superiority, has nothing but loathing for the rebels and all that they represent. He speaks of them as "miserable-looking men: the worst sort of ignorant yokels. . . . All the human dregs of the country are rising to the top. . . . Never before had I seen in one place so many ignorant-looking, poverty-stricken fellows. Like the mob at the burning of Henry Wade's house, they were pock-marked, furtive-eyed, slack-lipped, shambling, hoarse-voiced. Their laughter, when they laughed, was abrupt and flat, or like the crackling of thorns beneath a pot." And still again: "I've been watching them on the streets in the last few days, cursing and spitting at everyone that's got on decent clothes."[1] Yet it is these "spitting and cursing" yokels that triumphed over the person and the ideas of the polished and dignified Oliver Wiswell.

In my years of travel in Europe and Asia I have heard so-called Russian Whites—men and women of breeding, culture, charm, very much like the Oliver Wiswells in the days of the American Revolution—speak in words almost identical of the Russian "yokels" who had swept over them and forced them to flee as fast as they could and wherever they could, for their very lives.

This is no attempt to make a comparison between the American and the Russian Revolutions. The times are different, the peoples are different, even more so are the ideas and purposes involved. Aims in the American Revolution which have become sanctities in American life—the

[1] From *Oliver Wiswell*, by Kenneth Roberts, copyright, 1940. Reprinted by permission of Doubleday, Doran & Company, Inc.

right to private ownership, for example—the Russian Revolution has repudiated and destroyed. The violence of the American Revolution, in spite of the angry complaints of the Oliver Wiswells and their descendants, does not match the terror of the Russian Revolution, indeed it is like a burning bush compared to a raging forest fire. The one thing above everything else that is common between them is the hate they have aroused in their immediate enemies and in other contemporaries who have deemed their respective revolutionary aims and methods as assaults on their own beliefs and on their persons.

The Cavaliers in England spoke of Cromwell and his Ironsides in language no less vehement than Oliver Wiswell speaks of the "yokels" of his time. To this day Cromwell is more than anathema in Ireland, and "a Cromwell curse on you" is a part of the profane vocabulary of the Irish. The French Royalists likewise had only words of hate and thoughts of murder for the rebels of the French Revolution, and for excellent reasons. These rebels had deprived them not only of their privileges and their possessions but often enough of their lives. Men fighting each other in a revolution are always brutal. The revolutionaries have nothing or little to lose, and their enemies, whoever they are, have much or everything to lose. Therefore the fighting spirit of both rises to a feverish height. Hence the roughness and the toughness of revolutionary armies or of the armies of revolutionary countries. They think and fight in unorthodox ways. They do not abide by precedent, not always even by military precedent. They are ready for violent innovations, in the legislative chamber as well as on the battlefield. They are gamblers *par excellence* with their own lives as much as with the lives of others. In the case of the Red armies the fire of the Revolution has added enormously to their fighting strength just as the fires of earlier times added enormously to the fighting strength of the American, the Cromwellian, the French revolutionary armies.

However unacceptable Sovietism may be to the American people, in aim and method, in the light of the performance of the Red armies it is obvious that it was not its destructiveness but its creativeness that has given the Red armies their unexpected fighting strength. Creativeness in industry, in agriculture, in military science, in military preparedness, in education—with emphasis on science and mechanics, on the stirring of the new, even while killing the old, consciousness in the people; it is this creativeness which has built up Russia's military weapons and has made the Russian "big stick" the military miracle of the present war if not of all times. No matter what the fortunes or misfortunes of the Red armies when Germany again unleashes her loudly heralded offensive, their performance during the first nine months of fighting has more than astounded the world, the Germans more than the Allies.

So intense was Hitler's contempt for Soviet creativeness and for the new consciousness of the Russian people, that he never bothered to woo them through his usual high-sounding fake promises. He would "liberate" them from "Bolsheviks" and "Jews" was all he would allow himself to say to them. It had never occurred to him that a peasant in the darkest village might want to know what he would be liberated for. Hitler's appeal could readily evoke a response, and a hearty one, in the Russian White Guards, whom his adjutants had been grooming for Quislings, but never in the vast and highly Sovietized masses inside Russia, especially in the youth, who had come to regard Fascism as the meanest and most barbaric form of capitalism.

"Hitler and the Nazis," says a Russian appeal, "have contempt for all races except the German. . . . Who owns the land in Germany? The Duke of Coburg owns 25,000 acres; the Duke of Friedrich Anhalt owns 72,000 acres; the Count von Arnim-Muskau owns 64,000 acres; Marshal Goering owns 50,000 acres. And these dukes, counts, and barons have decided to seize the Russian land as well." And again: "They incite the Flemish people to kill the Walloons; the Croats to kill the Serbs. They set Ukrainians against Russians, then they kill the Flemish, the Croats, the Ukrainians; they compel the Norwegians to speak German and the Czechs to write German. They compel the Poles to groan in German as they are tortured to death."

And again, in an editorial in *Pravda,* the leading Bolshevik daily in Moscow: "Hitler takes on himself the task of restoring the rule of the landlords of Czarism, the destruction of national culture, and of the national governments. . . . It is his intention to turn all these people into slaves of German barons and landlords."

Barons and landlords, especially German barons and

landlords! For over a century and long before there ever were Bolsheviks in Russia or anyone had heard of them inside or outside of Russia, the Russian peasantry had been taught by ceaseless and impassioned underground propaganda to regard landlords and barons as their and the world's direst enemies. Under the slogans: "Down with landlords," "Down with boyars [gentry]," the Cossack, Stenka Razin, had led a sanguinary uprising of peasants and so did another Cossack named Yelemlyan Pugatchev. Whatever the grievances of the Russian people against the Soviets and however severe has been their ordeal in the years of Soviet rule, they could be depended on to rally in the battle against barons and landlords, especially against German barons and landlords, even as they can be depended upon to rally in battle against the more feudal barons and landlords of Japan.

Hitler's grudging and short-lived regard for collectivization, for example, did not significantly change the irreconcilable clash between the Soviet and the Nazi way of life and the Soviet and the Nazi temper. One reason for the extraordinary fighting morale of the Russian people in this moment of crisis is the universal, almost intuitive consciousness of this undying clash and of utter impossibility of compromise.

This consciousness is compounded of an array of convictions, sentiments, urges, that embody and yet transcend the ordinary definition of patriotism with its love of land, of home, of people, of government. It is further fired by concepts which the Soviets have inculcated and which are

almost lacking in other peoples that have fought and been
conquered by Hitler, which indeed are so inimical to
these conquered peoples, except to certain groups among
them, that were an attempt made to impose it on them,
they would battle against it to their last gasp, even as they
are now battling against Hitler.

First and foremost of these new concepts bears on the
subject of private enterprise. Nazi propagandists and ora-
tors never cease to proclaim that Nazism seeks the destruction of capitalism and the enthronement of Social-
ism. In his speech of January 30, in speaking of World
War I, Hitler said that "all capitalists of the time, as today,
threw all the weight of their influence into the scale in
behalf of war." He and other Nazis denounce capitalism
almost as loudly as do Bolsheviks, but only in words. Their
actions in all occupied lands, especially in those inhabited
by Slavs, demonstrate only too flagrantly that their all-
embracing aim is to oust natives from ownership and to
put Germans in their place. . . . They seek the destruction not of capitalism but of non-German capitalists, so
that only Germans shall become the capitalists as well as
the rulers of the world.

In all conquered countries German corporations, banks,
trusts have been assiduously swallowing native enterprises
and so have German individuals, especially Goering and
Von Ribbentrop. In its economic aspects the "new order"
that Hitler seeks to foist on Europe means, especially to
the Russian, the perpetuation of the most parasitic kind of
capitalism, because with it goes the brutally ancient ideol-

ogy of superior and inferior races and the right only of the superior races to be masters and capitalists.

But in Russia the destruction of private enterprise has been the mainspring of the Revolution. It is the rock on which Sovietism, its ideological framework, is grounded. Anyone who has lived through the campaigns of this destruction will forever remember the passion, the cruelty, the decisiveness with which it was realized. During the years of military communism at the beginning of the Revolution men were shot for selling privately a pack of potatoes or a sack of grain. During the first Five-Year Plan which witnessed the annihilation of NEP and the final thorough-going onslaught on private enterprise in the city and the village, no person in Russia was deemed so gross a sinner, so vile a criminal, as the immediate or one-time owner of a business of his own, whether a large manufacturing plant or a struggling village grocery shop. Deep into the consciousness of the people—especially of course in the youth, that is, those twenty-nine years old and younger, and of whom there are over one hundred and seven millions in Russia—has sunk the concept of the utter wickedness of private enterprise. This is the very core of the Soviet idea, and it is well always to be mindful of it.

Not that Russians wouldn't like to have good homes, good food, all the luxuries they could command. Most certainly they would. But they have been inoculated with the notion that only through collective ownership can and should such rewards be achieved. In all my wanderings in Russia I have never known a medical student who might want to engage in private practice or an engineering student who hoped to be the possessor of a factory of his own. Even if he cherished such a wish he would not dare admit it, perhaps not even to himself. Former businessmen who survived the liquidation of capitalism would pale or grow wroth at the mention of the possible return to their old pursuits. Never again would they want to endure the torment and the degradation of another "liquidation." Even priests in the Orthodox church have wholly absorbed the doctrine of the sinfulness of capitalism and preach it continually. As for the Baptists and the Evangelicans, the two leading Protestant sects whom the Soviets have found hardest to deal with, they had always been champions of co-operative economic effort though under their own instead of Soviet control.

The propaganda has been reinforced by feverish, everyday actuality. Not a factory or enterprise anywhere, even if only a village tavern or a roadside food stand, but has been built or taken over by the Soviets and operated by them. Too vivid ever to be forgotten are the memories of the sacrifices that people have made for every lathe, every engine, every brick that has gone into the new factories, or "the industrial giants," as Russians so boastfully speak of them. Butter, cheese, eggs, white bread, caviar, fish, that they and their children should have eaten; textiles and leather that should have supplied them and their children with shoes and clothes, were shipped abroad and sold at low prices when necessary, lower than those of others, so as to obtain the valuta with which to pay for the foreign machinery and the foreign services. Countless and gruesome have been the offerings that the Russian people have been called upon to make for their new economic order, in which collectivist or Soviet ownership has smothered all private enterprise.

To the worker the Sovietized factories are the very basis of his existence and of every hope and every ambition he has ever cherished. The overwhelming majority of them have never known what it is to work for a private owner, especially a foreigner, whether an individual or a corporation. They can conceive of no greater calamity than to be under obligation to do so. They have come to look on the Sovietized enterprise and the Soviet state, as has everyone else in the country, for the gratification of everyday needs and the fulfillment of a long-range goal, whether it be the purchase of groceries and clothes, the building of a home, the education of a child, the advancement of a career. They know of no other *rightful* or *righteous* way of living. Therefore they would rather die than submit to a system of private ownership, especially when Germans and Fascists are seeking to impose it on them.

True enough Russia is fighting a nationalist war; the peasant, as always, is fighting for his home and for his land. But the Russian nationalism of today is rooted in the concept and the practice of Soviet or collectivized control of "the means of production and distribution," even as Japanese nationalism is rooted in the concept of Emperor worship. The peasant of today is no longer the muzhik of yesterday or of the Napoleonic times. Sovietism, especially the three Five-Year Plans, have shaken out of him his old mentality. The concept of home and land no longer embraces the village hut and the individual allotment, least of all subservience to a landlord. Home now can mean only the collective farm, large-scale and highly mechanized. There is no road back to the old village and its old ways of life, however much some of the older generation of peasants might pine and long for it, except through blood and death greater by far, because of the machine with which the collective is armed, than the initial transition had involved.

The peasant who once knew only the wooden plow and the wooden flail or at most the light one- or two-horse steel plow, is now confronted with the fifteen- or sixty-horsepower tractor, the gang plow, the combine. Indeed the old peasant, whom we encounter in the writings of Tolstoy, Chekhov, Chirikov, and other literary luminaries, is gone almost completely. Hardly a shadow of him falls over the Russian lands. The young peasant, when in the army, drives a tank, operates an anti-tank and anti-aircraft gun, and other complicated mechanical weapons. He also, like the factory worker, has been reared in the new idea with its utter degradation of private enterprise—not usable private property, I must emphasize, which is continually encouraged, but income-yielding private enterprise. He too can only stand up and fight and die rather than allow foreigners—above all German Fascists, the most brutal of "capitalist exploiters"—to take over the collective farms and run them for their personal emolument. Indeed it cannot be too assiduously proclaimed that anyone who would seek to restore private enterprise in Russia, whether along Nazi or other lines, would lay the foundation for a struggle far more sanguinary than was the Soviet civil war and the accompanying campaigns of liquidation, and with far greater loss of life. . . . To appraise the Soviets in any other terms is to miss completely the temper and the passion of the Russian people in this moment of war and crisis, even more completely than did the Allied diplomats and generals—the diplomats far more than the generals—who in the early years of the Soviets had sent expeditionary forces to Russia in the hope of rallying the masses into an overthrow of the Revolution. . . .

Judging Russia solely in terms of Sovietophobia—of which Hitler is the leading exponent—or in those of the mentality of the Russian White Guards in Berlin, in Paris, in other European capitals—to whom present-day Russia is as alien as it is to himself—Hitler had counted on an internal breakdown which would facilitate the conquest of the country. Ignoring completely the hold of the Soviet idea on the Russian mind, he waged his ideological campaign with the usual Nazi weapons precisely as he had done in other countries, setting up one group against the other, one section against another. He strove to incite the Ukrainians against the Russians, the peasants against the Soviets, everybody against the Jews. Even while despising Slavs and all other races and nationalities in Russia, he sought to inculcate in them his own and Germany's racial hates against the races and nationalities among whom or with whom they had been living. But the universal massacres of Jews on which he had counted, the nationwide outbreak of other groups against each other which had been a part of his hopes and his plans, never materialized. The civil war, which was to disrupt and destroy the Soviet system and the Soviet idea and with it the Russian nation so that its lands and its possessions could easily be acquired by Germans for their own benefit and exploitation, never broke out. All Nazi appeals fell on inhospitable soil, evoked only wrath and deathly defiance. Instead of the internal breakdown which Germans and others had for years been prophesying—and never so much as in the months preceding the German onslaught on the Russian lands—Russians, of all races and nationalities, united as never before in Russian history, solidified their energies and their weapons in the fight on the German invader.

With no less unity and energy will they fight the Japanese armies.

CHAPTER III

The Power of Organization

I KNOW well the Ukrainian cities of Kharkov, Poltava, Kiev. I have visited them again and again. It is heartbreaking to think of them in ruins. Kiev especially makes one feel sad. Here is one of the most historic cities in Russia, citadel of Ukrainian and Russian nationhood. It is a city of hills and gardens, of trees and flowers, of museums and churches, among the oldest and most beautiful in the land. In external appearance, in its spirit of gallantry, Kiev represented, to me at least, the florescence of Russian and Ukrainian culture. It abounded in a warmth, an intimacy, a charm, a gayety which I found in no other Russian city.

In the worst of times—as after the civil war, and despite the destruction wrought by endless fighting and endless change of hands by invading armies; despite, too, the swarms of homeless and hopeless children at railroad stations, parks, cemeteries, doorways of eating places—it boasted a physical dignity in the very trees in the streets, the lofty spires of the churches, which made one forget the horrors of yesterday and the miseries of today. Here was a city that loved life and laughter, song and gayety.

Yet as in the case of the mighty dam that spanned the Dniepr which winds majestically around its towering hills, when faced with the necessity of retreat, the Russians forgot history and sentiment, beauty and art, remembered only the enemy, their hate of him, their resolve to inflict on him all the death and destruction they could, and so with their own hands they turned much of it into ruins. They could have made it an open city, as the French had done with Paris. They could have saved much of its glory and grandeur. But the passion to punish the enemy transcended all other considerations.

On entering the city, the Germans proclaimed loudly and joyfully to their own people and to the outside world that they had achieved a stupendous victory and a highly coveted war prize. Yet some time later, when American correspondents were taken on a trip to Kiev by the Nazi Ministry of Propaganda, they found the city a heap of smoldering and exploding ruins. Machinery in the many new factories had either been carted away beyond the reach of the invading army or was smashed and burned. Days after the evacuation, time bombs which the Russians had concealed blew up blocks of buildings. Nobody in the world, least of all the Germans, had suspected the thorough preparation which the Russians had made to dynamite the cities and factories which they could not hold. Berlin reported at the time that German engineers

and assisting crews had removed over 200,000 bombs of
one kind or another! The number that had blown up
couldn't, of course, have been reported, for the men who
were caught in the explosions never lived to tell. Door-
knobs were turned, bells were rung, hatchways were
raised, switches were lifted, and in response came thun-
dering explosions.

The Kreshatshatink was Kiev's main street. Evenings it
swarmed with the gayest young people in the country, the
sturdiest youths, the prettiest girls. The German commander moved into one of the leading shops on this street.
German officers made themselves at home in other buildings near by. A motion-picture theater, one of the best in
the city, had become their exclusive place of entertainment. Yet one evening, a few days later, the commander's
headquarters, the officers' homes, the exclusive motion-
picture haunt, expoded into dust and smoke.

Nikolayevskaya was another renowned street in Kiev.
Here were the Continental Hotel, which served the best
meals in Russia, the circus Franko, the city theater. Mines
of powerful force blew them into ruins. Retreating Soviet
soldiers and remaining Soviet guerrillas had performed the
task of destruction only too well. Factories, barracks, hospitals, restaurants, theaters, apartment houses, the newest
and most up to date, none were spared. Again I must emphasize that neither Hitler nor the German General Staff
had imagined the Russians would show such fiery hate of
them or would be in possession of such immense quantities of explosives, or would display such skill in organizing

the devastation of their cities. Nor did anyone else, least
of all the foreign diplomats and foreign military attachés
in Moscow. Excepting the American colonel, Faymonville,
not one of them manifested the least respect for Soviet
power of organization.

The story of Kiev, however, demonstrates only too vividly not only the immeasurable will to fight, but the inordinate amount of organization that has made possible
the effective fulfillment of this will. The outside world—
and Germans in particular—had assumed that Russians
were congenitally bereft of the gift of organization, in construction as well as destruction. They certainly were no
match for the Germans, so it was universally believed,
even among some older folk in Russia. One reason for the
profligate predictions inside and outside of Germany of the
imminent collapse of the Red armies after only a brief
period of fighting was because of the prevalent belief that
Russia's talent for *disorganization* would make her a
ready and helpless target of Germany's highly organized
and murderous fire power. Decidedly the skill with which
the Russians have been carrying out the scorched-earth
policy, particularly in the destruction of factories and
cities, if nothing else, amply testifies to the falsity of the
widespread assumption.

In part the misconception is a result of the unwilling or
the unseeing eye of the foreign observer, particularly when
in his everyday contacts with Russian officials and other
Russians he encounters shocking evidence of inefficiency.
In part it is also the outcome of a deliberate Soviet effort

to conceal the rapid acquisition of a new skill in work and a new competence in large-scale organization, especially when it is even remotely associated with national defense.

In the summer of 1936, on my arrival in Moscow, I went to see the press chief of the Foreign Office. I told him that I was contemplating a lengthy journey in the Ukraine, the Crimea, White Russia, with a view to observing fresh developments on the collective farms. I asked for the letter of identification which his office had always given journalists when they went on trips to the country. He informed me that he wouldn't give me such a letter. He was a new man, fresh from diplomatic service abroad, and I thought he had not yet familiarized himself with Moscow procedure, so I replied that without the letter a foreign journalist was likely to invoke suspicion and encounter difficulties, perhaps serious trouble, and besides in all the years I had been visiting the Soviet Union letters of identification had been freely given to journalists. The press chief remained unimpressed and persisted in his refusal. Presently he and I found ourselves involved in a hot verbal skirmish, neither showing special consideration for the person of the other.

But it was of no avail. The coveted letter I didn't receive. Rummaging in my papers, I found the one I had obtained the year before and so I used it. The new ruling was obviously intended to discourage foreign journalists from extensive travel. Nor was this the only new ruling. On leaving Moscow I stumbled into another, even more annoying. Before leaving a town or village I had to inform the police where I was going. The police wrote the name of the place in my passport and if in the course of my journey or even while waiting for the trains at the railroad station I changed my mind and decided to go elsewhere, which often happened, I was barred from doing so. If I violated the regulation I was sent back to the place from which I had come. It was all upsetting and exasperating, yet no one would disregard the new ruling, neither the Foreign Office in Moscow nor the police in the most far-away villages.

Why these annoying rulings? It couldn't possibly have been because conditions in the country had worsened and the Kremlin didn't want foreigners to see the deterioration. The summer of 1936 was the brightest Russia had known since the coming of the Soviets. Collectivization had begun to show the benefits of the application of modern science and the modern machine to the land and had rapidly mended the wounds of the famine of 1932–33. In Moscow the services had so conspicuously improved that a housewife could go down to a shop on her own block not only in the daytime but at midnight and buy butter, cheese, fish without the need of standing in line. People were better shod, better clothed, and were in the best humor I had known them to be.

There was much talk of the constitution, of civil liberties, of the "fruits" of "socialist democracy." Kulaks and priests were reinstated in citizenship and their children were accorded the right to attend high schools, colleges, universities.

Why, then, the new curbs on travel and investigation for journalists and for other foreigners?

The answer is Hitler and the Japanese. Both were becoming extraordinarily powerful, especially Hitler. He had spoken of German possession of the Ukraine, the Urals, Siberia. The Japanese had become equally articulate though not so loud as Hitler in their threats, and had followed up their words with insidious border clashes. The Kremlin more than took to heart the menacing pronouncements of the enemy in the west and of the enemy in the east. Hurriedly and quietly it unfolded fresh campaigns of military preparedness and just as at present, while fighting the German armies, it has converted every available amount of productive energy into the manufacture of ammunition, at the sacrifice of the daily needs of the people, so at that time it had striven universally to relate, directly and indirectly, every civilian pursuit to military preparedness. But it did not want news of it to get out of the country.

In official pronouncements it was always melodramatic in its praise of the invincibility of the Red armies. It was deluging the world with percentages as to the amount of mechanical equipment and flying and firing power it was rapidly amassing. But it always withheld detailed information, and it rigidly prevented diplomats and journalists from acquiring it. It wanted journalists to send out stories of which it approved, but it withheld or dismissed accounts of military preparedness in the everyday pursuits of the people.

On collective farms there was more parachute jumping than ever before, there were more aviation clubs, more lectures on guerrilla warfare, more classes in topography and military tactics, more target practice, more glider flying, and, what was equally significant, more storing away of food reserves and ammunition in strategic places. There were also more tractor drivers than ever before, more schools to teach still more youths the operation and the mechanics of tractors, and Moscow with its melodramatic love of secrecy didn't want the outside world to know it, not any more than it could help. Again excepting the American colonel, Faymonville, I knew not a single foreign military attaché in Moscow—nor a single diplomat —who had the least understanding of the monumental military preparedness that had been set in motion all over the land, and particularly on the collective farms.

Late in the summer of 1936 I was in the Kuban among the Cossacks. Moscow had just witnessed the trial and the execution of Kamenev and Zinovyev, two of the foremost leaders in the early years of the Soviets. But the people in the Kuban were neither excited nor visibly concerned about the event. It seemed far removed from their everyday life and burdens. Tragic a chapter as it might have been in the history of the Soviets, it evoked surprisingly little comment. The Cossacks were too absorbed in the fresh developments that were taking place all about them, the new machinery that was arriving in an endless stream, the new crops they were cultivating, especially cotton, which they had never before grown in the Kuban, and many other new aspects of agriculture.

I wanted to visit my native village in White Russia. Students in the University of Leningrad from there had told me that I wouldn't recognize it because it had changed so in the few years since I had last been there. Many new buildings had been erected, they said, and the land was worked with tractors, and there was talk of pulling down the old thatch huts and building a "socialist town" in squares, with a park, an athletic field, a clubhouse, and other community institutions. I was eager to go there, but the police wouldn't permit it. All of White Russia had become a gigantic armed camp, and they didn't want any outsider to see it!

Logically the Kremlin should have been glad to send out information that would impress potential enemies with its gathering military strength. But that is not the way the Kremlin mind works. With its passion for secrecy, it didn't want the outside world to know the nature of its strength, still less the manner in which it was acquiring it. Once, while spending a few days in a sugar factory in the Ukraine, I was particularly impressed with the water system that had been newly built under the supervision of a young girl, a recent graduate from an engineering school in Moscow. I snapped a picture of the dam and the falls and instantly someone appeared before me and took away the film.

At another time, while on a collective farm, I was intrigued by a new road that had been built to the cow stables, and I snapped a picture of it. Again someone leaped up, as if out of the earth, and asked for the film.

Tourists to Russia know only too well how vigilant is the watch on railroad stations, bridges, office buildings, so they won't be photographed. Beginning with 1936, I was no longer permitted to take pictures of young people on collective farms having military drill or parading with guns or practicing parachute jumping. "But that," I once argued with a Cossack militiaman, "will only show your enemies how strong you are, and you want them to know that so they will be afraid to attack you." He shook his head and muttered the inevitable and forbidding, "Nelzia."

In many other ways the Soviets were concealing the military significance of momentous changes in policy. Well do I remember the dismay and the wrath of radicals and liberals at the time the Soviets scrapped the old and introduced the new marriage laws. Divorce had become difficult and expensive. Birth control, while still legal, was frowned upon. Literature on the subject had disappeared from newsstands and bookshops. Abortions were banned, and the ban was rigorously enforced. Large families were not only encouraged but heavily subsidized. The official explanation of the sudden swing from something like free love to rigid puritanism was that the old law, with its tolerance of abortions, was ruining the health and the dignity of women; also in a socialist world women owed it to themselves and to society to let nature take its course without interference from man. This explanation contradicted everything that Soviet spokesmen had previously written on the subject of marriage, divorce, abortions, and the family.

One evening I happened to be at a dinner party with Gronsky, one-time editor of *Izvestia,* the official Soviet newspaper. Gronsky has since been purged, but at that time he was an important figure in Soviet journalism. I told him what radicals and liberals outside of Russia were saying about the new decree—that it was reactionary, and intended to raise more and more cannon fodder for the Kremlin. A hardened revolutionary with a record of life-long underground warfare against Czarism, Gronsky showed no offense at the language I used. He laughed and urged me to go on with my complaints, which I did readily and eloquently, repeating the violent language that I had heard among foreigners in denunciation of the new law. When I finished he said:

"We are such hardened sinners that abusive language has no effect on us. We shake it off like the flies that buzz around us. You and your kind are thinking of theories, and we are thinking of blood. Don't for a moment imagine that Fascism, the vilest form of capitalism, will permit us to go on unchallenged. Hitler, Mussolini, the Japanese, perhaps even the British, the French, and your own American capitalists, will attempt to crush us. They are trying all the time. Look at the Japanese and the way they keep shooting at us from across the Manchurian border. Of course we shoot back, and we're better shots than they—because it's our business to be better shots than anybody else. We've got to be prepared with weapons at least as good as the Fascists have, and in the long run the birth rate of a nation is a mighty weapon. Don't fool yourself into thinking it isn't. When war comes we may have to sacrifice three, four, five, yes, ten, and perhaps twenty years' births, millions and millions of our people, and we would be fools not to take advantage at this critical time of our biological potentialities."

Gay and versatile, Gronsky, on finishing his comment, picked up the guitar and started to play and sing Siberian revolutionary songs. He would say no more on the subject. Perhaps of a sudden he had become conscious of talking to a foreign journalist and regretted having expressed himself so frankly. In the *Izvestia* which he edited he would no more print the explanation he had given than propose turning over the Moscow automobile factory to a private corporation. Officially no people in the world have been more close-mouthed than the Russians on the subject of military preparedness.

The reinstatement of the Cossacks is another case. Foreign diplomats and journalists who were in Moscow on November 6, 1936, will long remember the celebration they attended in the State Opera House. It was the eve of the anniversary of the Revolution, and for the first time foreigners were invited to attend the event. They sat in boxes on one side of the house, and the Kremlin personalities, after the business part of the gathering was over, crowded into the boxes on the other side.

As far as I know this was the first time since the coming

of the Soviets that foreigners were in such close proximity to the all-powerful Politbureau, the ten men who rule Russia, and other high-ranking members of the Communist party. A lavish entertainment was offered to the audience, and to me the most impressive number was the Cossack choir, made up of Don and Kuban Cossacks, several hundred of them—men, women, and children. They were dressed in their ancient and resplendent costumes including the inevitable belt and dagger. They sang and danced, and so superb was their performance that every number evoked tumultuous applause. Stalin and Voroshilov sat beside each other in a box and applauded the chorus more heartily than anyone else. Every so often Voroshilov sent a note to the stage requesting the repetition of a song.

To me it was all so incredible. I had traveled at length in the Cossack *stanitsas,* and up to the summer of 1935 I had heard more laments there than anywhere else in the country, and with good reason. The Cossacks and the Soviets had fought one another with all the hate and violence both could muster, as readers of Sholohov's superb novels have learned. Yet now here they were—Don and Kuban Cossacks, men, women, and children—singing and dancing in the Moscow Opera House before an exclusive audience of foreigners and high-ranking Soviet leaders, the highest in the country; with Stalin and Voroshilov, who had led many a military campaign against them, applauding more heartily than anyone else. Here was one of the great reconciliations in Russian history and in the Russian Revolution.

At that time there were foreign radicals in Moscow who were no more pleased with the reinstatement of the Cossack than they were with the new marriage laws. They saw in it a further departure from original aims and a betrayal of the Revolution—a swing toward Fascism. If a native said so, he disappeared. If a foreigner said so, he was ignored. But the Kremlin was thinking of Hitler and of the Japanese. Both had been threatening war. Both were growing formidable in military power. Russia, the Kremlin felt, but seldom said so, might have to face both of them in battle at the same time. Therefore it would leave no element of military strength unexplored and unexploited. So it brought back the Cossack. In the light of the events since the outbreak of the war it was one of the most far-sighted measures the Kremlin had taken. For centuries the Cossack had been one of the most redoubtable soldiers in Europe, the supreme cavalryman. In the last war there was no soldier that the German dreaded so much as the Cossack. "Die Kazaken kommen" was an expression of this dread.

So the Cossack once more became a part of the Russian army. He got back his uniform, his saber, his dagger, his horse. The stanitsas were livened up with gay color and resounded with martial songs and with the wild gallop of men on horseback.

Now we know that in the recapture of Rostov and in the battle of Moscow in 1941 the Cossack played a decisive part. On December 5, 1941, the Germans were uncomfortably close to Moscow. With their binoculars they could see the city. They were already fighting for the honor of being the first regiment to enter the city and parade in the Red Square. According to credible authority Stalin communicated with the Cossack commander and told him to attack. The commander plunged into action in the sector which he was holding. Seven times he was repulsed with heavy losses. In the eighth plunge he stormed German strongholds, bent back the German line, and the retreat started. The commander died from his wounds, but after that, with the coming of winter weather and with the comparative paralysis of tanks, the Cossack, who is the mainstay of Russian cavalry, kept on driving the Germans back all along the vast-stretching battlefield. Of course he no longer fights only with the saber. The machine age has equipped him with new weapons. He carries rifles, machine guns, light artillery, hand grenades, gasoline bottles for the destruction of tanks—at times complete infantry outfits—so that if necessary he can come off his horse and join infantry units.

Foreign military observers, Germans in particular, remained unimpressed with the return of the Cossack to the Russian army. The next war, they predicted, would be won, not by horses, but by engines. Cavalry wouldn't be of much use; tanks would slaughter the horses and the men on their backs. Therefore the Reichswehr did not bother to cultivate much cavalry. The Russians paid no heed to this talk. They didn't neglect the engines. But they also cultivated the horse, and when the deep snows came, their policy was more than vindicated.

The introduction of rank into the army was still another departure from revolutionary practice that had roused widespread and loud protest among radicals and liberals outside of Russia. Here was further evidence, was the charge, of betrayal of the Revolution, of a swing to the right, toward Fascism, for only Fascists gloried in the display of uniforms and in according rank to leadership in the army and in civilian life. Once officers got back old titles—lieutenant, captain, major, colonel, general, marshal —they would, so it was further held, in time bring back the old ideas which would only further debase the Revolution.

Shortly after the reinstatement of the old titles, eight leading generals were shot. But the restoration of rank couldn't have been the cause of the execution because scores, hundreds of civilian leaders were also executed. The reinstatement of titles was purely a military measure, designed to strengthen the morale and the discipline in the army. Timoshenko might have proven the brilliant general that he is even if he were known only as a commander of an army instead of a marshal and had worn a less stylized uniform. The same may be said of General Gregori Zhukov, of General Boris Shapozhnikov, of the other generals who have won distinction in the war against Germany. But the appeal to the ego of the officers and the new powers that were vested in them made not for weakness but for strength in the army.

By far the most extraordinary and least recognized civilian weapon of national defense was collectivization of the land. Achieved at a gruesome cost in substance and life, it had roused more denunciation in the outside world and in the foreign colony in Moscow than any other Soviet measure. This is not the place to discuss the subject. I have done it elsewhere in great detail.[1] But again excepting Colonel Faymonville, now a brigadier general and one of the most close-mouthed and most astute observers in Moscow at the time, there was not a single foreign diplomat, not even among the Germans, who beheld in collectivization any military significance or anything save madness and ruin. One young official in the German Embassy, whose name was Schiller, an agricultural expert, readily perceived, in spite of the Kremlin's errors and the newly stirred strife in the villages, the agricultural significance of collectivization. But after Hitler's ascension to power, Schiller did not remain long in Moscow.

The Russians, of course, never hinted at the military aspects of collectivization and thereby lulled foreign observers into a complete disregard of this feature in the vast and violent agricultural revolution. They stressed only its farming and social implications, which, of course, in the long run are primary.

Yet without collectivization they never could have waged war as effectively as they have done. Its contribution to Russian military strength—in organization, in morale, in actual fighting and firing power—is beyond calculation. In its beginnings, when famine had swept the Ukraine, when the older peasantry especially saw in it only doom,

[1]*Hitler Cannot Conquer Russia.*

many foreign journalists and diplomats denounced it as serfdom and barbarism. There were Russians too, even Communists, who in those days hated it and predicted collapse. But the Kremlin remained unmoved. In time the modern machine healed the wounds, and since then collectivization has transformed not only Russian agriculture and the Russian village but the peasant. It has enabled the government to direct the production of crops and to keep control of output in its own hands. It has brought the machine age to the many-millioned peasantry and within a short space of time, in less than a decade, it has made the once wood-minded muzhik, especially the young generation, mechanically-minded, engine-minded, tractor-minded, and thereby prepared a vast army of recruits that could easily master the tank, the anti-aircraft and anti-tank guns, and all the other latest and complicated weapons of warfare. It has trained masses of women in the operation of large-scale, mechanized farms, which is the essence of collectivization, so that they could tend to agriculture, as they are now doing, while the men went to war. It has brought target practice within the reach of every man and every child in the village and has trained millions of sharpshooters who never cease to harass Germans in their rear. It has made children in the most remote countryside as vigilant against possible fifth columnists and enemy parachutists as adults and has taught them, too, how effectively to deal with both. It has aided enormously in the transport of troops, food, and ammunition to the front. With its numerous large buildings it has proven a ready shelter for the wounded and for the millions of refugees who fled in the wake of the German occupation. It has made possible a needed degree of efficiency in the solution of the pressing problems, not only of war, but of work and rest, of order and discipline. Above all, it has prepared the people not only for an invasion, but for an occupation, and has taught them the most dangerous and the most terrifying of all modes of warfare—guerrilla fighting.

If Nazi parachute troops have met with universal defeat and disaster in Russia; if Nazified Ukrainians, especially intellectuals from Galicia and other parts of Europe outside of Russia, in their attempt to organize fifth columnists and saboteurs against Soviet armies in the Soviet Ukraine, have suffered a similar fate, it is because the collectives since their earliest days have taught the people, even children, not only vigilance, but methods of detecting and annihilating these and other plotters. Again and again school children have discovered German parachutists in fields and forests and have either shot them with their own guns or hastened to summon older folk for the deadly reckoning.

The notion that Russia has a genius not for organization but for disorganization clings stubbornly to the mind of the outside world, as the writings on Russia even in recent years so eloquently demonstrate. Yet the facts presented in this chapter, which is concerned chiefly with the military preparedness of the civilian population, unfold a spectacular concept of large-scale organization. It is the newness of the concept that has baffled and infuriated the outside world.

In the light of what is happening on the Russian front and in spite of the lag and neglect in the everyday social services, it is obvious that the three Five-Year Plans have, among other things, served as one of the most amazing efficiency schools the world has ever known.

CHAPTER IV

The Power of the Machine

A DISTINGUISHED American editor, after a stay of several weeks in Moscow and Leningrad, in the best hotels of both cities, remarked half in jest, half in earnest, "Russia never can have a good army because her plumbing is so bad." By American standards Russian plumbing is worse than bad; it is execrable. It is, in fact, one of the most orphaned institutions in the country. It is never mentioned in industrial reports, in the voluminous treatises on the various Five-Year Plans; not significantly anyway. It is not a part—not yet—of the Russian mentality, any more than it was in the old days. I am not speaking of the widely traveled individual Russians, of whom there never have been many, but of the broad masses of the people.

In the years that I have been going to Russia I have had requests from Russians for American seed catalogues, fashion magazines, agricultural bulletins of universities and of the Department of Agriculture in Washington, for medical reports, automobile catalogues, but never for any literature on plumbing. The subject hardly existed for them.

During my stay in Novosibirsk, the capital of western Siberia, whenever I visited the Soviet office building I was always impressed by its rugged simplicity and its bright spaciousness. But whenever I had occasion to observe the plumbing I felt more than disconcerted. Yet the rifles of the young people who were daily practicing sharpshooting in the rifle ranges of the city were superb. This was the opinion not of an amateur like myself, but of a German diplomat whom I met in Novosibirsk, who had been an officer in the German army during World War I. He hated Bolshevism and the Soviets, but he had been on many hunting expeditions in Siberia and he was lavish in his praise of Russian guns and of the skill young Russians were acquiring in handling them.

There is no doubt that the condition of Russian plumbing has had something to do with the universal belief on the outbreak of the Russo-German war that the Russian armies would swiftly be defeated. For people, including diplomats, even those who had seen service in Russia, reasoned, if the plumbing in the country is dilapidated or non-existent then the millions of Russian soldiers couldn't competently handle tanks, anti-aircraft guns, and all other highly mechanized military equipment, and would be no match against the German army, made up, as it was, of men skilled in the use of modern machinery and modern fighting and firing weapons.

Little did such people realize that since the earliest days of the Soviets neither food, nor clothes, nor shoes, nor houses, nor water closets mattered as much as guns. The specter of war haunted the country by day and by night and so had the problem of preparing it for a victorious fight. The "big stick" consumed its chief thoughts and energies.

Sigrid Undset, the famed Norwegian novelist, winner of the Nobel prize for literature in 1928, in her recent book, *Return to the Future,* in which she describes her experiences in Russia while on her flight from beleaguered Norway to the United States, tells that on learning at the Stockholm airport that she was to travel to Moscow on a Russian plane she felt "uneasy." Friends of hers who had participated in the Finnish war had told "harrowing stories of the Russians' dealing with modern machinery of every kind; as a rule they knew nothing about how to handle it and were too careless to be disturbed by the fact that they knew nothing."

The time was July 13, 1940, three years after two groups of Russian fliers had astounded the world with their non-stop flight from Moscow across the North Pole to California, a distance of over 6,000 miles; twelve years after a Russian ice breaker and airplane had picked up in the far North the remnants of the ill-fated Italian expedition under the command of Nobile; six years after the sinking of the boat, *Chelushkin,* in the icy waters of the Sea of Okhotsk and the spectacular rescue by plane in the midst of gales and blizzards of the one hundred and four members of the expedition and of all the dogs; in other words, after many record-breaking and dramatic exploits of Russian fliers, especially in the Arctic regions, which demonstrated that Russian pilots possessed more than average mechanical competence.

But legends die hard, especially when only a short time earlier they had been facts. I too was once a victim of the "uneasiness" of which Madam Undset speaks. I flew from Erivan to Tiflis, a short journey by air lasting only one hour. But the year was 1935, the plane was an open two seater of an ancient model, the terrain one of the most mountainous in the world, and the pilot a young Georgian girl! Yet it was one of the safest air journeys I have ever made.

Russia's outward appearance has always been dramatically deceptive. "It is the Goddamnedest poorhouse I've ever seen," said an American businessman on his return to Moscow from a lengthy journey in the south. Madam Undset echoes these sentiments though in less picturesque language. She saw in Moscow "indescribable filth, dilapidation, wretchedness in *all* the houses in which they live [my italics]. . . . I did not see *one* Russian who smiled except the attendants on the trans-Siberian railroad. [Madam Undset's italics] . . . not *one* woman with leather shoes on her feet. [Madam Undset's italics.] . . . What I had had no previous idea of was the stench in Moscow . . . in Moscow every place is a slum."

The words sound familiar enough; I have heard them over and over. Yet I must confess that even in the worst times, as during the first Five-Year Plan, I had not only seen Russians smile, I heard Russians laugh, multitudes of them, and quite gaily: in school yards, on skating rinks, in college dormitories, in the homes of people, and of course in the theaters. In those times Russians, in the privacy of their homes, laughed with special heartiness at themselves, as the countless anecdotes that freely circulated in the country so abundantly testify. Together with Elmer Rice, the American playwright, I attended in Moscow the opening performance of Charlie Chaplin's *Modern Times,* and what particularly impressed us about the audience was its uproarious mirth. "Just like New York," we said to each other over and over.

Also in those other sad and bitter times, in the early twenties, shortly after the end of the civil war and the famine, even in most remote villages in the Tatar country along the Volga I had seen more than *one* Russian woman wear leather shoes, even in summer, when out of habit, owing to economy as well as to comfort, peasants prefer going barefooted, and when girls in the cities, because of their absorption in physical culture, prefer light sandals to leather shoes.

In Moscow and all along her journey across Siberia, Madam Undset is impressed by Russian ruin, Russian chaos, Russian filth—this in the summer of 1940, a little less than a year before the Russo-German war. In justice to the distinguished novelist, it must be stated that she readily confesses, "I am so constituted by nature that nothing Russian can awaken a sympathetic response in me."

All this is well enough. But if Russia were only the kind of country that Madam Undset pictures, how then is it possible that the Soviet armies are the only ones that have been able to fight the Germans on their own terms? After all, the German armies are the most mechanized in the world, have at their command the best and the latest weapons that the modern machine shop and modern engineering can perfect. Ruin, chaos, filth create neither planes nor tanks nor the ability to operate them; least of all do they create the will to fight as savagely as the Russian armies have been fighting and as gallant a readiness to die. The question applies also to those writers, editors, diplomats, who because of the terrors of the Revolution, of the spirit of martial law under which Russians have practically been living since the coming of the Soviets, of the hardships and miseries they have endured, see Russia chiefly or exclusively as a land of blood and horror.

Admittedly Russia gives the impression outwardly of a poorhouse, though millions of people do laugh when there is something to laugh at, as when someone recites Gogol or Dickens; millions more, really untold millions, not only soldiers, but civilians, do have leather shoes, even in most faraway villages. Admittedly the dictatorship has been ruthless, even as Cromwell was ruthless, with friends no less than with enemies, when they rose or attempted to rise or were suspected of rising or of wanting to rise in opposition. Admittedly Americans and Britishers would fight to their last drop of blood against such dictatorship, and so might Russians, had they shared the experiences, the education, the economic and political elevation of the American and British peoples in the last one hundred and fifty years. Had this been so there might never have been a Russian dictatorship—most emphatically not of the kind Sovietism is. Admittedly also France was no dictatorship; she enjoyed civil liberties such as Russians to this day know only on paper; France boasted the finest restaurants and cabarets in Europe; the best-dressed women who always wore shoes of finest leather and of latest styles; the plumbing too in the hotels in which foreigners lived was superb. Paris was no "stinking slum" like Moscow, but was a city of cheer and fragrance, of brightness and comfort.

Yet the German armies swept over Paris and over more than half of France with the swiftness almost of a hurricane. In their defeat the French, thrifty, freedom-loving, highly individualized, had not bothered to destroy or damage their factories, their crops, their oil tanks, their artillery guns, their mines, their steel shops, their armament factories which are among the best in the world, their railroads, their bridges, their highways. One reason why Hitler is so powerful that he can wage war on many fronts and hold in subjugation all the conquered countries, including Madam Undset's homeland, is because of the enormous booty he has gathered in France, at the expense, of course, of the French. Were he to win the war, neither France nor Norway will again attain the freedom and the prosperity, the brightness and the cheer they had known. If he loses the war and the conquered countries including France and Norway recover their bodies and their souls, it will be essentially because of the fighting, the sacrifices, the killings of these Russians who live "in indescribable filth," who never smile, and whose women, at least in Moscow, so Madam Undset tells us, never wear leather shoes, not *one* of them!

How like the pronouncements of Oliver Wiswell on the depravity and on the degradation of the American rebels!

It is, of course, never any use to appraise Russia in terms of Norwegian, French, American, or any other Western standards, least of all in terms of the resentments and the hates which Soviet destruction of private enterprise, Soviet atheism, Soviet dictatorship have aroused. Russian history, I must repeat, has been different from that of any Western country. The Czechs are Slavs and the Russians are Slavs. Originally the two started out as the same tribes, the same people. Yet drifting west, the Czechs, in the course of the centuries, have benefited materially and in- tellectually from the stream of Western civilization, from their own magnificent Jan Huss, from the Renaissance, from the Cromwellian revolution, from the Reformation, from the French Revolution, and from all that these imply in terms of science, the machine, liberal thought, standard of living, all of which had barely touched Russia.

Century after century, despite Austro-German repres- sion, the Czechs had been rising higher and higher in their social and political development, while the Russians, with the exception of a small group of weeping noblemen and anguished intellectuals, had remained largely shut off from contact with Western enlightenment and Western refinement. Hence the differences between Czechs, all Western peoples, and the Russians. Indeed Russia can be understood solely in terms of her own past and her own present feverish struggle to emerge at enormous cost in comfort and life as a modern nation, with a modern standard of living; above all with modern weapons of war, with a "big stick" that can strike a telling blow at so advanced and formidable an enemy as the German army.

At present the material standard of living is conspicuously poor in Russia everywhere, but experience in the handling of the modern machine is sensationally rich, even in the tundras of the polar regions and in the outflow of the Gobi Desert. It is not so rich as it is in America, not universally, but is infinitely richer than it was prior to the year 1928. In this one respect alone, so momentous in time of peace, so decisive in time of war, the three Five-Year Plans have transformed Russia beyond recognition. Otherwise the mammoth Soviet military machine would long ago have crashed on the dirt roads or bogged down in the deep snows.

The world is astounded at the amount of weapons and other equipment that Russia has brought into play in the fight against Germany: tanks, heavy and light artillery, automatic guns, hand grenades, Molotov cocktails; planes of all kinds, four- and six-engined bombers, light snub-nosed reconnaissance ships; all manner of bombs; superb winter outfits for the soldiers, millions of them; tractors, motor trucks, also sleds, light and heavy ones, for the transport of armament, food, other supplies.

Hitler has complained that he had no inkling the Russians had amassed such vast quantities of armaments. All the more remarkable is this achievement when it is remembered that until 1929 the Russian steel industry was centered chiefly in the Donetz basin in the Ukraine. Nearly all the new armament industries have been erected during the three Five-Year Plans, or within the past thirteen years, not counting 1942, which is supposed to be the last year of the third plan. Throughout these years guns had taken precedence over butter and boots, over shirts and suits, over plumbing and water closets, over a multitude of other necessaries which the people desperately wanted and for which now and then they clamored neither too humbly nor yet too boisterously. Had they had their butter and their boots, their shirts and their suits, their plumbing and their water closets, their ease and their comfort, and not their guns and the other highly mechanized war weapons with which to match those of the Germans, nor their factories strung along their immense spaces, especially in Asia, for the manufacture of these weapons, they would have been in the same plight in which the Poles now find themselves—beaten and anguished serfs of the most barbaric anti-Slavs of all times.

With their blood, at the behest of a ruthless dictatorship and in a surprisingly short time, they have carried the modern machine in as advanced a stage of development as their knowledge and their means would permit, to the most faraway regions of their far-flung lands. With their blood, and again at the behest of a ruthless dictatorship and in a surprisingly short time, they have acclimated their fingers, their eyes, their minds, their very souls, to the requirements of this machine, so that they could handle it, the tool of work as well as the weapon of war, with the care and the competence that it deserves. Other things didn't matter. The services in the shops, the restaurants, the hotels, the railroads didn't count. The style of the shoe, the dress, the suit of clothes was of no consequence. Not even soap and handkerchiefs were of any moment. Without the ownership and the mastery of the machine, so the leaders, from Stalin down to all of his opponents, kept repeating over and over, in voices never soft nor ingratiating, always harsh, almost terrifying, all might be lost: the country, the nation, the Revolution, the very lives and most emphatically the future of the many millioned masses. With the machine all could be won, especially the future. So everything in the country was sacrificed for the enthronement and the mastery of the machine. Its power in this moment of battle for sheer survival is unquestioned. Like the power of the new idea and of the new organization it is saving the Soviet Union from dismemberment and extermination by Germany.

It will save it no less from attempts at subjugation by Japan.

CHAPTER V

The War of Values

In the summer of 1933 an American woman of Quaker origin came to Moscow with a letter of introduction. One evening we went to the Park of Rest and Culture. We strolled about the flower-bordered pathways watching the crowds of young people at play. Of a sudden the lights went out and from the distance rose loud military commands. Amid the flares that were thrown up we could see an army coming toward us—crawling on its belly, jumping, kneeling, crawling again, shooting, pushing closer and closer in our direction. It was the military maneuvers of boys and girls of high-school age. My companion was aghast—mere children, she said, training for war with rifles, machine guns, and other military paraphernalia! At that time the war was so remote to the outside world, especially to Americans, including this writer, that the thought of it sounded absurd. Foreign diplomats and foreign journalists in Moscow beheld in Russia's war

feverishness no more than emotional hysteria, or a scheme
to detract the people from immediate difficulties and miseries, or downright paranoia. Some there were who said
that Russia was teaching even school children to shoot,
so that they too could participate in the plan to impose
revolution on the outside world at the point of a gun.

But foreign public opinion and foreign denunciation, as
always, left the Kremlin and its followers neither shaken in
their convictions nor regretful of their tireless preparedness.
War was their supreme concern, and never was it so clear
and meaningful as now, and therefore all over the country boys and girls of high-school age, like their older
brothers and sisters, like their fathers and their mothers
too sometimes, were undergoing military drills like the
one we were witnessing. Had they not done so throughout the past years, they never could have fought the Germans with the kind of soldiers they now have—still less
with the people's army they have evolved—in the front
and in the rear. The guerrilla never could have become
the mighty warrior that he now is. He would have had
neither the audacity nor the competence that he is so
brilliantly displaying. He is the superb fifth columnist—
in the enemy's line and even more in the enemy's rear.
He is the disrupter, the panic monger, the incendiary, the
killer. Ghostlike he hovers everywhere, over general no
less than over private. He is a woman, a boy, a girl, a
grandfather, a grandmother, sometimes a child of only
eight or ten. His consuming passion is to destroy the invader, the worker no less than the junker, the peasant no

less than the Gestapo agent. Knowing the forest as he does and the swamps too, and inured to the cold, the gale, and the blizzard, the ice and the snow banks, he can hide from sight and yet see the world before him, sometimes with his own eyes, sometimes with the eyes of someone else, a woman or a child, and aim his torch and his bullet with deadly precision.

In the Russian literature of the future for hundreds and hundreds of years to come, and whatever the social order in Russia, the guerrilla will be the supreme hero of this war more even than he was in the civil war, just as in Russian and in Norwegian, Dutch, French, Belgian, Polish, Czech literature of the future, for hundreds and hundreds of years to come, the German will be the supreme villain.

After nine months of fighting, the Russians know only too well that the war is not finished, that Hitler is mustering a powerful army for an offensive in which he will attempt to strike a crushing and final blow, so that never again will he have to face a winter campaign in Russia. If there is no internal breakdown in Germany—and there is no visible or audible sign of it at this writing—Hitler will succeed only too well in gathering an army of fresh millions—sturdy and well-trained men and youth—and hurl them once more against Russia.

Industrially he commands a stupendous advantage over the Soviets. At his disposal are all of Germany's gigantic industries; also those of France, Poland, Holland, Norway, Czechoslovakia, Belgium, and of the other con-

quered countries. At his command are hosts of the most
brilliant engineers in the world, also millions of the most
skilled workers in Europe, Germans and others. Unlike
the Russians, he has not been obliged to blow up with his
own hands a single blacksmith shop or set afire a single
home in any of the conquered countries or in Germany.
Air raids have been a nuisance and have wrought damage
here and there but neither fatal nor crushing. "Almost the
whole continent of Europe," wrote General Hermann von
Hannecken in an issue of the periodical *The Four-Year
Plan,* "is forging arms which Germany needs." Raw materials, manufacturing energy, labor power are being
brilliantly co-ordinated and organized with a view to
whipping out the maximum amount of production. Hitler
knows only too well that time is his most implacable
enemy and he must not let it run away from him. Every
minute counts, even as every scrap of brass and nickel
and copper and paper and wood counts. If the statue of
a Rousseau has to be melted, well and good. If other
statues of non-German heroes and idols need to be flung
into the furnace, nothing must intervene to stop it. German workers and women and even children are promised
magnificent rewards if only they will work more and more
assiduously and grind out the mountain of weapons and
armaments that the Reichswehr must have to strike the
Russian armies with a view to overwhelming them.
Schooled as the Russians are to estimate the fighting
powers as well as the standard of living of nations in terms
of coal and iron, steel and copper, oil and electric power,

they are only too keenly aware of Germany's stupendous manufacturing energy and of the flaming effort now to make use of every particle of raw materials, of every ounce of energy, human and mechanical, to achieve the armament superiority which is Hitler's only hope of wiping out the disaster of his Russian campaign.

And of course he has all the motive in the world to seek a reckoning with the Red armies. Made up of people whom he and other Nazis have branded as "swine," "vermin," "beasts," "Mongol degenerates," he must wipe out the military reverses and the stigma they have inflicted on his army, his name, his prestige, his ideology. To allow such people to attain victory over "the superior race" is to invite immediate doom and eternal disgrace.

To Hitler a victory over Russia is as indispensable to political survival as air is to physical life. Never can he justify his ideology, never can he realize his far-flung aim of conquest, without the subjugation of Russia. In July 1939, shortly before the outbreak of the war, as I strolled along the main streets of Danzig I saw the windows of bookshops cluttered with displays of newly printed books on the Ukraine. These books described in graphic language the Ukrainian climate, resources, rivers, forests, minerals, the fat lands, and all the other glories and treasures of this part of the Soviet Union. The aim of these books was obvious—to stir enthusiasm for this land of promise which was to be German *Lebensraum* forever and ever, and on which Germans by the millions were to get land for new houses and a new life.

Without Russia, Hitler cannot hope to fulfill the extravagant promises he has made to his people in the years that he has been dominating the German scene. He cannot offer them "the life of plenty" on which they had been counting—the new farms, the new homes, the new businesses, the new markets, the new pleasures, the vast new world of riches and happiness. The banks of Germany and the industrial corporations as well as individual Nazis have already swallowed generous amounts of loot in one form or another. Germany now dominates not only the politics but the finance, the industry, the trade, the agriculture of the conquered countries. Several million common folk have already benefited from German conquests and now live in homes, on farms, run shops and trading posts from which natives have been driven. All of Gdynia, for example, the most modern Polish city and the most prosperous, is now occupied by Germans. Warsaw, Cracow, Radom, Lodz, Prague, Bratislava, Wilno, Riga, Tallinn, Kaunas, and many other cities in the conquered lands, are now being settled by Germans who get their reward at the expense of the natives, for fealty to the Führer, or for the sole reason that they are Germans.

But the vast masses of other Germans are still only making sacrifices, more and more all the time, without reaping any of the sumptuous rewards they have been promised. Nor can these promises be fulfilled without the conquest of such a huge and rich country as Russia. Only after such a conquest and with the expulsion and extermination of masses of Russians in Europe can Germany hope to lift her population to the figure of two hundred million which Hitler deems indispensable to the maintenance of German supremacy. Thus without a Russian victory, now or later, Nazi ideology has no firm rock on which to lean, and Nazi conquest of Europe, not to say of the world, remains a taunting chimera.

Yet, however formidable his military strength in man power, in armaments, in fighting morale, in military leadership, now less than ever has Hitler any chance of winning this victory. Despite eloquent boasts and lavish promises, he cannot conceal from the German people the tragedy of the Russian campaign during the winter of 1941–42. Directly and even more indirectly and quite dramatically, the German press and even Goebbels go on disclosing the magnitude and poignancy of this tragedy. On September 1, 1939, Hitler had assured the German people that war between Russia and Germany in 1914 was a mistake and never would it happen again. He wouldn't allow it to happen, he vowed. Yet in the Christmas issue (1941) of *Das Reich,* Goebbels' weekly journal, there is this fatal revelation: "Almost every one of us had a difficult letter to write during the past few months in order to tell somebody's parents or somebody's young wife that we share their sorrow and that we shall always cherish the memory of their son or of her husband." What a world of meaning which no juggling with casualty figures can conceal is contained in the simple phrase, "almost every one of us"! Equally revealing and unexpected is the further admission in the same article in *Das Reich* that "nobody knows as yet when Germany will reach the gate behind which lie the new century and a less painful age." Nobody —not even the Führer!

Consider the revelation in the order of the High Command early in February 1942, about "last sons." A family that has already "offered a high blood sacrifice," which in other words has already lost several sons in the war— two, three, or more—will have its last son, if he is on the fighting front in Russia, withdrawn from combat duty to a less perilous task. From this order alone the German people and the outside world can judge of the high casualties that the Reichswehr has sustained in the Russian war—casualties, I must repeat, which Germans had been assured by the Führer over and over they never again would be called upon to endure. "Why are you for Hitler?" I asked the porter in the hotel in Danzig. "Don't you know that if the Führer comes here there will be war and you or your son might be killed?"

"Ach!" came the confident reply, "you foreigners don't understand. The Führer knows how to get the things he wants without fighting. Leave it to him." Such was the widespread faith in the word of the Führer among Germans not only in Germany, but in other European lands.

Meanwhile the ideological superstructure of Nazism rooted in the concept of Germany's racial or human superiority is being shaken. No matter what the victories Germany may still attain over Russia, the fact that in the initial onslaught the Reichswehr had failed to equal Napoleon's triumph over Moscow cannot help but loosen the foundations of this superstructure. The admission of some Nazi spokesmen, however grudgingly made, that the Russian soldier is as good as the German, is tantamount to a confession that Germany's superiority is a legend, for according to Nazi standards the chief test of superiority is in the battlefield.

Amusing yet significant is the comment of the *Nazional Zeitung* of Essen: "After all, German soldiers are not like the Siberians whom we discovered early one morning fast asleep in the middle of the road after a night with twenty-five degrees of frost." If German soldiers cannot duplicate the feats of endurance of Siberian soldiers, then certainly they cannot be superior to the Siberians, even if the Führer tells them they are superior to everybody.

Never again, in my judgment, will Hitler have the fanatical armies that he had first flung against Moscow. Flushed with faith and triumph, the Hitlerite youths who made up the bulk of these armies are either dead or enduring hardships which they never imagined they would be destined to face in Russia or anywhere in the world. The army that Hitler is gathering for the new offensive will never believe the assurances, should they be made again, that within three or six weeks they will be in Moscow, Russia will be at their feet, England will be deprived of her last ally in Europe and will be obliged to sue for peace on Germany's terms. The presence of America in this war, if nothing else, will preclude such belief. The new German army will know what happened in Russia during the winter of 1941–42, in part from personal experience, in part from conversation with participants in the Russian campaign. It will know that the pick of the Reichswehr at the height of its fighting powers, in men, in equipment, in morale, in generalship, and long before the arrival of real winter, had failed to wrest Moscow or Leningrad from the Russians and had to withdraw from Rostov, gateway to the Caucasus, with its rich manganese mines and its still richer oil fields. It can never march under the banner and with the passion of invincibility with which the first army marched into Russia. It will know too well the vengeful powers of the Russian earth and Russian humanity.

It will also know that in Russia the German soldiers who had preceded them had found none of the loot that they had scooped up in other conquered lands, especially in rich and goods-glutted France. In Russia there was no pork, no bacon, no coffee, no canned foods to send home to the family; no silk stockings, fashionable dresses, woolen scarfs, ornate household goods with which to gladden the heart of a mother, wife, or sweetheart; no mattresses, blankets, pillows, sheets, or other household articles which the rich Polish population in Gdynia was obliged to leave behind for German settlers and German soldiers. In Russia not even the Führer or the Gestapo could find gold, diamonds, platinum, or foreign securities. Indeed the new German army will know that Russia is the only country Germany has invaded which has paid neither the cost of the invasion nor of the occupation, and has not even supplied enough food for the invading armies. The Russian scorched earth had left for the advancing German armies a much more battered and desolate land than Hitler or the High Command had anticipated. In the places from which the Germans have had to retreat, the earth was made even more desolate by German bombs and the German torch. The army that will carry on the new offensive will march through a more miserable Russia than did its predecessor. This will neither cheer nor comfort the men though, of course, they will fight with energy and zeal. The threat of retribution and massacre in Russia and elsewhere will spur their fighting zeal perhaps to madness or desperation.

Yet the men in this army will know that instead of fifth columnists, saboteurs, collaborationists, which in other countries have been lured into aiding them—little men performing menial tasks as well as men in highest position in politics, industry, finance—in Russia they will find at every turn guerrillas trained in military tactics, above all in sharpshooting.

No less significant is the lesson the Germans have learned and are still learning about prospects of colonizing Russia. Alfred Rosenberg may have moved to Kiev with a large corps of assistants to organize the conquered territory and to plan the settlement of Germans in the Ukraine at the expense of the native population, but he and his assistants as well as the German soldiers have learned only too well the murderous hostility of the local population. The arrival of German colonists in the Ukraine will be a signal for increased guerrilla action. The torch will be busy and so will be the rifle and the ax. Blood will gush freely, from German colonists as well as from Russian guerrillas. Fired on by Moscow's secret emissaries who filter freely into the conquered countries, the colonists, if or when they arrive, will be subject to constant and murderous revenge. They will come, of course. They have never yet refused to go whenever or wherever the Führer has ordered them to do so.

From a Russian viewpoint this *is* a battle unto death. Despite stupendous losses in life, in equipment, in territory, in factories, the Soviets are in possession of formidable fighting resources. Man power is no problem. Russia is essentially a land of youth. According to the census of 1939, out of one hundred and sixty-nine million population, one hundred and seven million are twenty-nine years of age and younger; one hundred and thirty-two million are thirty-nine years of age and younger. Colonel Nikolay Klimov of the General Staff declared at the height of the German advance that, despite the loss of large sections of the population, Russia could mobilize twenty-seven million men for military duty. The one thing Russia has not asked of the Allies is man power. Millions of fresh recruits are being trained in Siberia, in Central Asia, and far behind the fighting lines in European Russia.

November 7, 1941, the day of the anniversary of the Revolution, passed off under verbal expression of sympathy for the German people. "Greetings," was the Russian announcement, "to the German people, groaning under the yoke of Hitler's blackguard bands. We wish them victory over bloodthirsty Hitler." In their radio appeals the Russians followed a similar mode of thought and speech. But the distinction which they draw between Nazis and Germans inside the Reich they fail to manifest toward the German soldiers and other Germans on Russian soil and associated with the invasion or the occupation. Against these Germans, regardless of their social origin, the Russian generals, the Russian press, the Kremlin spokesmen—including Stalin—thunder flaming hate. "No mercy to the German invaders," exclaimed Stalin in his speech of November 7, 1941. "Death to the Germans (on Russian soil)," he demanded. "The fact is," he went on acrimoniously, "that in their moral degradation the German invaders, having lost all human semblance, have long ago sunk to the degradation of wild beasts."

The depredations of German soldiers against Russian civilians; their constant appeals to the Ukrainians to rise up against the Russians and to Russians and Ukrainians to massacre the Jews; the eviction of natives from their homes; the looting of the depleted larders of the peasantry; the confiscation of warm clothes, especially of sheepskin coats; the seizure of hostages; the wholesale public executions have converted the conquered parts of the country into a scene of bloody reprisals.

Russian soldiers, civilians, generals, political leaders, including Stalin, know only too well that the German soldiers in Russia are largely peasants and workers, as Hitler has been boasting, or the sons of peasants and workers—

the very people on whom they had counted to paralyze the Nazi military machine when it was flung at "the socialist fatherland." Since the earliest days of the Revolution the Russian people have been taught that peasants and workers anywhere would have neither the will nor the heart to attack them. After all, Russia has no "capitalist exploiters." Instead, the German peasants and workers follow only too well the commands of the German generals and the Nazi Führer. Whether terrified by the Gestapo or mesmerized by the material reward which the Führer has held out to them, has indeed in places already given them—homes, for example, from which natives have been driven—they fight Russian peasants and workers on Russian land with a demoniac energy. True, when caught they are sometimes glad to show repentance. "We have had enough of this war," said one German war prisoner; "let fat Goering freeze here in the Russian snow." Sometimes they may even desert. But the fact that the German army is fighting well, "is clinging to every inch of land," as Stalin said on February 23, 1942, is full of meaning for Russians as well as for the outside world. From a Russian revolutionary viewpoint they have committed the most heinous offense against their own dignity, their class, above all against the "socialist fatherland," an offense which according to revolutionary justice never can be expiated save in death.

No wonder that on January 3 *Pravda*, in an editorial captioned "Mercilessly Annihilate the Fascist Beast," writes scorchingly: "Annihilate the German invaders like mad dogs. The Hitlerite beasts want to turn our land into a desert. We shall turn it into a death zone for Fascist dogs. . . . Not a single dog must escape stern punishment. . . ." In other words, anyone on Russian soil fighting for Hitler is a dog and a beast and must be killed. Anybody! "Fight them, annihilate them," *Pravda* demands. "Smash them. Soviet warriors, show no mercy." And the *Red Star,* official organ of the Red army, roars out a similar command: "Not a single German shall leave the Ukraine alive," which matches the appeal of General Gregory Zhukov: "Death to the German occupants."

Years ago in *Humanity Uprooted,* writing of the nature of the fighting if Soviet Russia were involved in a war, I said that it would be "the last word in human barbarism." It certainly is that in the rear of the German battle line in Russia even more than at the front.

Many Russian leaders are saying that this year will witness the end of Hitler and the war in Europe. Eduard Beneš, one of the most astute and highly informed diplomats, likewise predicts the end of the European war this year. He voiced this prediction at a time when the Germans were still on the offensive in their first onslaught on Moscow. There might be wishful thinking in these forecasts, though neither the Russians nor the Czechs are inclined to underestimate the burdens that they are still to face, military and others. They know only too well how formidable are the powers of the German armies. On February 8, 1942, Sir Stafford Cripps, former British Ambassador to Moscow, declared that the prospect of a German defeat "by this time next year" was no empty conjecture, provided the British lay aside private interest and "give Russia all the support" they can.

It cannot be too often nor too vigorously emphasized that after all that has happened on the Russo-German battlefield not even Hitler can keep aflame the doctrine of German supremacy and the corollary doctrine that it is the destiny of Germans to conquer, rule, and own the world. With this doctrine in process of dissolution and with the prospect of winning the rich and coveted *Lebensraum* they had been promised becoming more and more dim, even if they again push their way close to or even beyond Moscow and Leningrad, the German people and the German generals face too grim a future not to attempt to terminate the war sooner than might be expected if only the chance should present itself. Of course the dread of murderous retribution, especially on the part of the enraged Slav peoples, will be a powerful weapon in the hands of Nazi leaders and Nazi generals. But whether or not this year will witness the end of the war, it most emphatically will witness the decisive battles of the war, especially on the Russian front.

Much will depend on the events in the Far East. Sooner than she expects Russia may find herself at war with Japan. The fall of Singapore, Malaya, and Java is full of dire omen for Russia. Whether the new German offensive goes well or badly, Hitler will have all the reason in the world to persuade Japan to attack Russia in the Far East, so as to divide her fighting powers between two fronts, four thousand miles apart, before American and British industrial aid can reach the Soviets in vast enough amounts to offset the present industrial advantages of the Axis powers. Japan too, even if she suffers serious reverses but no collapse, will have her own motive for wanting to shatter the empire that Russia is so energetically building in Asia. Indeed she must shatter it if she ever hopes to achieve her ambition to become the mistress of the mainland of Asia.

II

The Great Test in Asia

CHAPTER VI

The War in Installments

Before we fight American imperialism," says Sinsaku Hirota, the Japanese military writer, in his book, *How We Are Going to Fight,* "Japan must secure for this war a base of raw materials in the rear such as is afforded by Manchukuo, northern Sakhalin (Soviet), the Maritime Provinces (Soviet), and if necessary the Amur regions (Soviet) and Baikal (Soviet)."

Language could be neither more explicit nor more meaningful. Nor is Hirota the only man in Japan who writes with such frankness and audacity. But the conflict between Russia and Japan long ago passed the border-line of mere rhetoric. The fact is, as already indicated in the opening chapter, that unofficially the two countries have been at war for nearly ten years. They have not broken relations; have not recalled ambassadors—not yet. But their foreign ministers have exchanged notes bristling with accusation, denunciation, and threat. Their press,

daily and periodical, has engaged in prolonged and vitu-
perative duels, and all along their far-flung borderline—
stretching for a distance of over two thousand miles—
their forces have met in many a bloody skirmish. Only
the war offices of the two nations know the precise number of these encounters. In 1938 the Japanese admitted
twenty-four hundred, and since then there have been
many more.

On three different occasions: in July 1937, in August
1938, in May 1939, and in three different places: on the
Amur River, on the hills of Changkufeng, at Lake Nomonhan on the border of Outer Mongolia, the clashes had
assumed the magnitude and ferocity of full-sized battles;
both sides bringing into action not only the bayonet, the
rifle, the machine gun, but the tank, the bomber, and
heavy artillery. The Japanese had initiated these battles
for two purposes—to test Russian military strength and
to ascertain whether Soviet armies could be easily defeated. At heavy cost they learned, especially in Changkufeng, where the battle had raged for fourteen days and
nights, and at Lake Nomonhan, where it had spurted on
and off from May to September, that Soviet armies could
more than hold their own. On both occasions the territories which Japan had set out to seize had remained in
Russian hands, the armistice terms, to the dismay of Japanese generals, acknowledging Russia's right to them. In
Changkufeng the Russians were supposed to remove their
flag from the top of the hill. They have not done so, and
the Japanese have made no attempt to pull it down.

Since then Japan has abandoned hope of an easy victory over Russia, unless, of course, Russia were disastrously weakened in a war elsewhere. But Japan has abandoned neither the ambition nor the hope of ousting her Slav neighbor from the Pacific area, deep into the heart of Siberia as far as Lake Baikal, and, if possible, all the way to the European border in the Urals. Nor have the Japanese made a secret of this sweeping aim. On the contrary, they have again and again given it loud and violent utterance, though seldom officially. The Harbin *Shimbun,* which is the spokesman of the General Staff of the Manchukuan army, bluntly declared that "our policy is to eliminate Red Russia from Asia. . . . The land east of the Urals and the Altai is Asia. It is the place for the expansion of Japanese culture. In that northeastern corner of Asia the influence of Japan must become supreme, and Japan must strive at least for the lands east of Lake Baikal. This is the slogan that is before the eyes of the Japanese. Our policy toward Russia is expressed in that slogan."

Nor have the Japanese ceased to proclaim their imperialist purposes even now while they are fighting the English-speaking world and Holland. On January 28, 1942, *Pravda* carried a flaming editorial under the title of "Divide Skin of Unkilled Bear," which was a retort and a challenge to the effusive talk in the Japanese press of a "Great Eastern Asiatic Economic Zone" that is to include eastern Siberia and Australia. "If Japanese journalists wish to occupy themselves with some kind of boastful bragging and bluff about war in the Pacific, if in spite of everything they want to divide the skin of the unkilled bear, that's their affair."

Russia, to the Japanese militarist, is not only a racial and ideological enemy but a formidable barrier to the realization of his ultimate aim, which at various times has been enunciated under different names, such as "Asia for Asiatics," "Pan-Asia," "The sacred mission of Japan to preserve peace in Asia," and more recently as "Greater East Asia Co-Prosperity." Whatever the name and however involved and academic the phraseology, its meaning has undergone but little change. Japan wants above everything else to establish herself as mistress of Asia, and Russia is in the way, on land, on sea, in the air, and getting more so all the time, all over her far-stretching Asiatic possessions.

The Japanese militarist cannot help saying to himself that victory over the sea powers whom he is now fighting, were it ever achieved, might be fruitless as long as Russia sprawls all along Japan's doorstep and is in command of a mighty land army, a substantial fleet of submarines, especially small ones, known as torpedo or suicide submarines, a powerful air force, an immense hinterland that is in process of feverish industrialization, and vast stores of ammunition all over the Far East, including dumps of incendiary bombs. As long as Sakhalin, Kamchatka, Vladivostok, Karaginskii Island—to mention only a few of the well-known Russian possessions in the Far East—remain in Russian hands, the Japanese militarist cannot feel secure in his powers and his conquests. He is apprehensive about the fate of Manchukuo, Inner Mongolia, and northern China, which he now holds firmly in his hands. Russia might make a push against these countries or might help China to do it, or might eventually unite not only with China but with India for this task. Indeed, with Russian bombers and fighting planes within two or three hours' flight from Tokyo and other large cities and industrial centers, the Japanese population has been taught to regard Russia, and only Russia, as the one nightmare that hangs over them and their everyday life and which their army, navy, and air force must sooner or later blast out of existence. "Four- and five-engined airplanes (Soviet)," says Natsuaki, "have as their objective the bombardment of Tokyo, Yokohama or Osaka, Nagoya and Kobe. . . . Japan cannot sleep peacefully a single hour. That is why in order to avert such a catastrophe it is necessary to strike quickly in the region of Vladivostok." This has been the theme song of the Japanese press, military and other, for over a decade.

The neutrality pact which Matsuoka concluded with Moscow in April 1941 is no more than a smoke screen, just as was the Russo-German non-aggression pact of August 1939. It is a prelude not to peace but to war, precisely as was the Stalin-Hitler pact unless, I repeat, Japan suffers a sudden collapse. Russia had wanted a non-aggression pact with Japan in 1932. When Kenkichi Yoshizawa was passing through Moscow on his way from the Paris ambassadorship to become Foreign Minister in Tokyo, the Russians approached him on the subject. They wanted the

pact desperately, so as to feel somewhat assured of peace in
the Far East while they were strenuously preparing for
the start of the second Five-Year Plan. Mr. Yoshizawa
took the proposal "under advisement." Later, on December 13, 1932, Alexander Troyanovsky, Soviet minister in
Tokyo, was informed that the time for it "was not ripe."

This is what the Japanese said publicly. Privately they
spoke a different language. In 1933 Matsuoka stopped off
in Moscow while on his way to Geneva to a conference of
the League of Nations. The Soviet Foreign Office held a
reception for him. Foreign diplomats, the foreign press,
and Russian writers, artists, and Soviet officials crowded
the reception halls. At that time Karahan, since purged,
was in charge of Russia's Far-Eastern diplomacy, and he
and Matsuoka withdrew to a corner and remained there
nearly all the time. Naturally we American journalists
wanted to know what the two diplomats were discussing
so intently and so secretly. But not a word did we learn.
Neither Matsuoka nor Karahan would hint at the subject
of their conversation. Only later it became known that
during his stay in Moscow, Matsuoka offered to sign a
non-aggression pact with Russia if in return Russia would
recognize Manchukuo. Firmly Russia rejected the proposal.

But this was a mild price for the much-wanted non-
aggression pact, compared to the one "the representatives
of business circles" of Japan drew up in 1933 at a conference at which Mr. Hirota, the Japanese Foreign Minister and formerly an ambassador to Russia, had presided.

The resolution which the conference had passed demanded among other things cessation of revolutionary propaganda in the Far East, repeal of Soviet labor laws by which Japanese concessionaires in Sakhalin had to abide, particularly with regard to the length of the labor day, which the Russians had reduced to seven and eight hours. Though Russia had already embarked on her second Five-Year Plan and had ruthlessly liquidated nearly all private enterprise all over the country, the Japanese further demanded the right to exploit Russian timber and mineral resources in the Far East on the basis of private enterprise. They also proposed that Russia withdraw all her troops from the Siberian Manchukuan border and turn over to Japan without compensation their legal rights to the Chinese Eastern Railway which they had seized the year before.

To the Russians these demands signalized an encroachment on sovereignty and an outright attempt of Japan to put herself into a strategic and military position for the occupation of the Maritime Provinces and for a drive eastward as far as Japanese military power would permit. Naturally, Russia repudiated all these private "feelers." Let it be emphasized here that throughout the years of the Soviet regime, whatever its dealings with foreign powers and however desperately it might be pressed for outside aid of one kind or another, it never entered into negotiations with any nation which involved the violation of its own sovereignty.

Therefore Japan's motive in signing not a non-aggression pact but a neutrality treaty with Moscow in April 1941, is no less meaningless than was Hitler's when he sent Von Ribbentrop to Moscow in 1939 to negotiate a more or less similar understanding. Like Hitler, Japan wanted to insure peace with Russia until other enemies might be disposed of. The incontestable fact is that the antagonism between Russia and Japan has converted their far-flung borderline into explosive armed camps that are ready, at a moment's notice, to crash into gigantic battle. Russia's geographic proximity, of which Japanese writers never cease to complain, looms as the most obvious and spectacular, but is not the sole, source of this antagonism. There are many others.

At one time during the Russian civil war Japan had virtually realized her ambition of pushing Russia deep into Siberia as far as Lake Baikal, as a subsequent chapter will disclose. Foiled in this attempt by Russian guerrillas and by American pressure, she changed her tactics and waited for a more opportune moment to attain the cherished end. She set out first to make herself mistress of all Manchuria, despite the Treaty of Portsmouth reaffirmed in 1925 by the Treaty of Peiping, which barred Japanese "influence" in northern Manchuria. This part of the country was to remain Russia's zone of "influence."

Russia's chief concern there was the Chinese Eastern Railway, which was built by the Czar in 1896. Some years ago I traveled on this railroad and I was astounded at the high quality of the service. Day coaches, sleeping cars, diners—the general air of comfort that pervaded the trains and the railroad stations exceeded anything I had known in Russia. The road had always been one of the finest and best managed in the world and was more than an agency of transportation—it was a vast and many-sided empire. When I was in Harbin the very word *doroga*—road—dominated the vocabulary and the economic and cultural life of northern Manchuria. It operated farms, shops, hotels, parks, resorts, schools, laboratories, medical services. It even maintained orchestras and bands. It was the great civilizing force in the country.

The management was under joint Russian and Chinese control. The arrangement was for the Chinese, if they so chose, to buy out the Russian share of ownership in 1939, or to continue the partnership until 1963, when it would automatically revert to their exclusive ownership. But in 1932, while fighting the Manchurians who resisted the sudden Japanese invasion, Japan pounced on the Chinese Eastern Railway and proceeded at once to establish her own control. She seized trains for the transport of troops. She confiscated rolling stock, arrested, jailed, beat up— sometimes shot—Russian officials and railroad workers. Accidents increased. Wrecks were frequent. The Russian press flamed with protest. The Soviet Foreign Minister kept up a barrage of violent indignation, but Japanese generals and diplomats remained unimpressed. Reaching the end of the first plan, Russia was too weak to take action, and the Japanese knew it. In May 1933 Litvinov offered to sell the road for six hundred and twenty-five million yen. The Japanese countered with the figure of fifty million yen. Accompanied by tumult and acrimony, the bargaining dragged on for two years, during which time the Japanese, so the Russians charged, were deliberately ruining the road so as to thwart competition with their own South Manchurian Railway and to degrade its value. On March 23, 1936, Russia sold it for one hundred and forty million yen. The nominal purchaser was the government of Manchukuo, a creation as well as a possession of the Japanese Government.

Japanese control of the road was not without political benefit to Russia. It quieted, at least in some quarters, the charge that the Soviets were imperialistic, otherwise they would have of their own accord abandoned a property built by the Czar whom they had overthrown and whose foreign policy they had denounced. Yet it was an immediate economic blow, and, even more, a military threat. It deprived Moscow of the short cut to Vladivostok, making it necessary for trains to zigzag over hundreds of extra miles along the winding Amur River, and, what was more serious, the Japanese hurried to the Siberian Manchukuan border 'a large army and soon enough were involved in quarrels and skirmishes with Russian forces. To the Russians these border skirmishes meant that Japan was poising for a thrust into eastern Siberia with a view to detaching it from Moscow. They had more than adequate reason for this conviction, for none other than General Khayasi, Minister of War, had announced that "the sale of the Chinese Eastern Railway does not alter the situation in the Far East." This, to the Russians, spelled further

Japanese aggression. So they in turn hastened to fortify themselves formidably all along the Manchukuo border in Siberia and in Outer Mongolia.

One reason for Japan's designs on Russia's Far East is the desire to come into possession of its wealth in natural resources. This territory is Russia's eastern borderland. It is of immense size—1,072,569 square miles, an area equal to one half of Europe or about five times that of Japan and Korea combined. It borders by land and sea on Japan and on Manchukuo. At one point it almost touches Alaska. Big Diomede Island in Russia's Far East is separated from Little Diomede Island in Alaska by about two miles of water. It is also washed by the Sea of Japan, the Sea of Okhotsk, the Sea of Chukotsk, and Bering Sea. Its coast line covers a distance of 10,400 miles.

The late Paulina Osipenko, an eminent woman flier, on her flight in the autumn of 1938 from Moscow to near Komsomolsk, was so fascinated by Russia's Far East that she wrote an account of it. In part this account is based on scientific records and in part on personal impressions.

"Stretching lengthwise," she writes, "and crosswise for thousands of miles, it affords a multitude of contrasts. This vast territory comprises both a subtropical littoral and the icy shores of Wrangel Island; the boundless fertile plains of the Amur Valley and the moss-covered ground of the Chukotsk tundras; the dense jungle of the Ussuri forests and the wild mountains of the Sikhota-Alin range; the rich valleys of the Ussuri and the virgin stretches of eternal ice."

With no little emotion she goes on to describe this vast
and little-known land. To her it is "a conglomerate of
climates and vegetation," where the dwarf birch and the
cork tree, the tundra brushwood and the Indian lotus, the
fir tree and the wild grapevine abound. Nor is the fauna
unexciting. For here live the gold pheasant and the ptar-
migan, "the tiger and the reindeer, the Himalayan bear and
the walrus, the Nepal marten and the fur seal." A country, therefore, not only of great spaces, great wildness,
great adventure, but of great riches as the following Russian table, with particular emphasis of its meaning to
Japan, graphically demonstrates.[1]

Natural Wealth of the Soviet Far East	Value Japan's Annual Imports, in Millions of Dollars
Coal, 200 billion tons	40
Oil, 285 million tons	140
Lumber, 8 billion cubic meters	50
Iron ore, 2½ billion tons	50
Zinc, 136 million tons	6
Copper, 135 million tons	10
Possible annual fish catch, 2½ million tons	Catch in foreign waters, ½ million tons

In addition there is also gold here. One third of the amount
mined by the Soviets annually comes from the Far East.
Here are also silver, platinum, sard, and auriferous crys-
tals. Then there are large deposits of marble, tuff, granite,
limestone, gypsum, and marl. In the waters of the rivers

[1] *When Japan Goes to War,* by E. Iogan and O. Tanin.

and the seas are seven hundred and thirty varieties of fish, some like the orc in the Amur, not found anywhere else, so Soviet ichthyologists report. Along the coast of Kamchatka, the Sea of Ohkotsk, there are whales, sea lions, sea calves, seals, walrus, white whales, and sea otters.

This is the general picture of the wealth and the forms in which it is found in Russia's Far East. The sources of the immediate and specific sources of conflict between Russia and Japan over this territory and its resources, we may as well start with the island of Sakhalin, one of the coal and oil treasures in the Far East. By the Treaty of Portsmouth, signed after the Russo-Japanese War, Japan obtained control of the southern half of the island, but the oil and the coal lie chiefly in the northern part. Russian geologists estimate that the oil reservoirs of Sakhalin amount to three hundred and forty[2] million tons—a highly coveted prize to an oil-thirsty nation like Japan. By agreement with Russia, Japan has been permitted to exploit half the oil fields and also half the coal mines in northern Sakhalin, paying rent, not in money, but in kind. Yet renting a concession is not the same as owning it—least of all to the Japanese militarist.

But the Soviets had no intention of leaving the exploitation of the oil and coal of Sakhalin exclusively to the Japanese. They started their own development—bored wells, opened gushers, also mined coal. In 1932 they launched the slogan, "To catch up with and surpass" capi-

[2] This figure is a result of estimates made later than the one shown in the preceding table.

talist nations in production, and the one place where they had unmeasured success in achieving this goal was Sakhalin. With their imported and highly modernized machinery and stinting neither money nor labor, they soon somewhat surpassed the Japanese in the amount of oil and coal they obtained. The Japanese sulked, argued, protested. They regarded Sakhalin as much a part of their *Lebensraum* as Germany does the Ukraine, and do not relish the prospect of Russia benefiting from its resources. They were not ready to seize it, for that meant war with Russia. But they would keep its resources as much as possible for themselves.

Quarrels over Russian fisheries in the Far East have added to the irrepressible conflict. Fish is one of the chief foods of Japan, taking the place of meat in European countries, and fishing is one of the leading occupations of the Japanese people. Of the three million fishermen in the world, about one half are Japanese, so the Russians estimate. They operate around 360,000 boats and account for at least a third of the world's annual catch. But it happens that Russia's waters in the Far East are rich in fish, especially in crab and salmon, for which in prewar days there had been a growing market in England and America. In 1875 the Czar of Russia had agreed to accord the Japanese the same fishing rights as his own subjects. In 1907, yielding to Japanese pressure, the Russian Czar accorded the Japanese special rights. During the time Japan had occupied Russia's Far Eastern territories, 1918–22, she had arbitrarily abrogated the treaty of 1907 and with the aid of naval craft proceeded to establish a monopoly of the fish in Russian waters. She built canneries on Russian land and brought new floating canneries into Russian waters.

Following the withdrawal of her troops, she concluded a convention with the Soviets, allowing her for a period of eight years, or until 1936, to make use of certain waters in Russian territories. Meanwhile, spurred by the need of food and for articles of export which would yield foreign money, the Russians proceeded to develop their own fishing industry. At the beginning of the first Five-Year Plan they had only one canning factory in Kamchatka; on its conclusion they had sixteen. In 1938 the number had leaped to forty-one. The Japanese were more than displeased. Not only were the Russians canning fish for their own use, but for export, competing with Japan in the markets of America and England. But there was no way they could stop the Russians.

Again and again in the disputes over fisheries the Japanese contended that fish was indispensable to their daily life, and that Russian restrictions of one kind or another would bring hardship and starvation to the Japanese people. To this charge the Russians countered with tables of figures showing that the fish in question, caught in Russian waters, "occupy first place in Japan's fish exports."

The quarrels were aggravated in 1930 by the closing in Vladivostok of the Bank of Chosen, a Japanese institution. The Russians charged that this bank was engaging in illegal speculation with Russian money. Under the impetus of fiery Anti-Russian propaganda, an attempt was made by a Japanese on the life of Anikeyev, the Russian trade representative in Tokyo. Anikeyev was seriously but not fatally wounded. The fact that the Russians had put up their own factories for the manufacture of barrels and other equipment which they had formerly been buying in Japan added to the intensity of the quarrels.

I was in Russia at the time, and the verbal lashings which Japan and Russia had been directing at one another made foreign journalists feel that war between the two might erupt at any moment. The Russians never failed to proclaim to Japan that they were ready for a military showdown. But Japan was not yet ready for an all-out challenge, and, despite continuous denunciation and acrimony on both sides, Japan in 1936 sought a renewal of the fisheries treaty for twelve years. After much bargaining and quarreling the Soviets had agreed to grant it and the details were fully worked out. The Japanese Privy Council had approved of the treaty, and it awaited the signature of the Emperor.

All was quiet on the eastern front, and then with the violence of an earthquake the quarrel burst out again. For some mysterious reason, perhaps at Berlin's instigation, Japan chose that very time—November 25, 1936—to sign the Anti-Comintern Pact with Germany and to make the act known to the whole world. To the Russians the pact meant a military alliance against themselves. Promptly they announced their withdrawal from the treaty. Under no circumstances, they said, would they sign it. Japan threatened war. Foreign journalists in Moscow stayed up nights and remained close to their telephones in expectation of exciting announcements. Again and again Japan threatened war. But the Russians remained firm. They did more—they ceased to make deliveries of pig iron to Japan and indicated to Japanese citizens in Vladivostok that their presence there was unwelcome and unwanted. They didn't hesitate to treat them with severity and to expel them.

Again Japan was not ready. Also she was afraid of America, which, though hostile to Bolshevism, might join in the war against her, and she wanted to avoid fighting a powerful navy and a powerful army at the same time. So in the end, at much loss of face, Japan contented herself with what the Russians were offering—a fisheries agreement not for twelve years but for only one.

Japan swallowed the hurt and bided her time, allowing her indignation and protest to express themselves in intensified border clashes and now and then in large-scale though unofficial fighting as at Changkufeng in 1938 and at Lake Nomonhan in 1939, where the Japanese, by their own admission, had sustained 18,000 casualties in killed alone.

CHAPTER VII

The Fight Goes On

A SURVEY of the relations between Russia and Japan, however impartially or exhaustively made, brings to the surface nothing but conflict at every point of contact at which the two nations touch each other. Only military considerations of the Japanese generals have thus far confined Japanese attacks on the Soviets to threats of conquest and to border clashes.

The Russians, of course, hold that however fundamental and violent their differences with Japan, a basis of agreement could be reached if only the Japanese would manifest an earnest desire for it. But no such desire has emanated from Japan. Now and then, if only for the sake of official politeness or to soothe the ruffled sentiments of an offended Russia, Japanese diplomats have given lip service to a desire for peace and good will between the two nations. But every such utterance has been more than offset by the violence of the rhetoric of other leaders, generals and politicians, and by the writings in the military journals and the daily press. Even more has it been negated by the hundreds of border clashes in which the Japanese army in Manchukuo has engaged the Russian forces in the Far East. The fact that few Japanese generals and politicians of rank think and speak of compromise and peace with Russia is of itself evidence, definite and conclusive, that Japanese leaders seek no such end. Emphatically they are girding themselves for only one way of settling their cumulative quarrels with Russia—by the sword, only by the sword.

Nor in the light of what Russia represents in terms of ideas and even more in terms of relations with her immediate Asiatic neighbor can they think otherwise. There is nowhere a common ground between Soviet and Japanese ideology and practice. The clash is formidable, hopeless. A country like Japan, in which finance and industry are largely centered in the hands of a small group of privileged families with an age-old feudal tradition, can only abhor Russia's attack on private ownership in finance, in industry, in trade, in agriculture. Emperor worship, the rock of Japanese nationalism and patriotism, is in complete conflict with Sovietism, which rose to power out of the deathbed not only of Czarism but of the Czar, his wife, and his children. To the Japanese, Emperor Hirohito is not only the lord patriarch, but the embodiment of the virtues, the powers, and the wisdom which the individual citizen or subject must revere. The sanctity of this concept is as deep seated in Japanese thought as its wickedness is in Soviet ideology. "It goes without saying," said Tanaka Chigaku, owner and editor of a widely circulated daily newspaper *Dai Nippon*, "that Nippon, founded by the gods, is a divine country. It needs no explanation that the elements entering into the organization of the state have naturally, within themselves, the minds of the gods and are destined to follow God's task." Since the Emperor is the head of the state as well as the nation, his divine origin is beyond scrutiny or question.

In a textbook on the national ideals of Japan extensively used in the middle schools, Yutaka Hibino reiterates these thoughts in language at once rapturous and mystical:

"What words can adequately describe our unique Empire unchanged and unchangeable, blessed on the one hand with a single immutable Imperial line and on the other with courageously devoted subjects, who ceaselessly fulfill their duties and overthrow enemies of the Empire. . . . The patriotism of our Imperial people is manifest in that keen endeavor to obey and respect the commands of the Emperor to the last and most minute detail. This ideal of service to the Throne is a special characteristic of our nation which exists nowhere else in the world." Most emphatically such faith in the divine origin of the Emperor and the demand for unquestioned fealty of the people is to the Soviet mind a form of crassest exploitation.

Not that Russian propaganda is powerful in Japan. It isn't. Thought is rigidly controlled and prescribed, and anything suggestive of Sovietism is rigorously banned. But the existence of the idea in itself is dangerous, so Japanese of influence feel, especially as it comes from a country which, as someone has expressed it, "rests its chin almost on the belly of Japan."

In a decisive and vehement way Sovietism also implies the dispossession of landlords, confiscation without compensation of their land and its free distribution among the peasantry. Such confiscation would deal a severe blow in the first place to the Emperor, not only to his prestige, but to his economic well-being, for he is perhaps the largest holder of real estate in the country, with especially large possessions in forest lands.

In his detailed study of Japanese agriculture prepared for the Institute of Pacific Relations, Andrei J. Grajdanzev presents a table showing that in 1939, 31 per cent of the agricultural families in Japan were owners of land, 26 per cent were tenants, 42.4 per cent were part tenants and part owners. Half of the owners held less than 1.23 acres, more than three fourths possessed less than 2.45 acres, and only 1 per cent owned more than 24.5 acres. "It is clear," says Grajdanzev, "that the vast majority of owners have tiny plots which resemble gardens rather than fields."

Indebtedness is another aspect of Japanese peasant life that aggravates the agrarian crisis, especially as interest rates are high—mostly 10 per cent or higher. Nor is it easy for a farm hand to become a tenant, or for a tenant to become an owner. In Soviet literature on the subject of Japanese agriculture the comparative landlessness and the heavy indebtedness of the peasantry, as well as the inability of the government throughout the years to do more than to ameliorate the condition of only a small percentage of them, through meager loans, are receiving constant attention and emphasis.

Not that an appeal of Russian Bolsheviks has any chance of inflaming the Japanese peasantry into an uprising. The rice riots in Japan were a result of a local impoverishment and not of external agitation. In the early years of Sovietism, when it was bristling with international fury and when it called on factory workers and landless peasants all over the world to rise up against property owners and property ownership, the Japanese peasantry evinced not the least interest in the appeal. There is no evidence that a significant number of them had heard of it. Besides, patriotic as it is, steeped in Emperor worship, in reverence for feudal usage, it would dismiss as absurd any counsel that might come from Russia, any Russia, Czarist or Soviet. The ancient distrust of Russia's good intentions not only persists but has become intensified. Widespread and violent is the propaganda among the common people, that Russia, because of Communism, is Japan's most nefarious enemy. "In one way or another," says Furuya Eichï, a Japanese Fascist spokesman, "sooner or later, Red Russia must be destroyed. That being the case, let it be destroyed by the hands of Japan in the Far East."

To the Japanese ruling groups, military and civilian, Moscow symbolizes the idea of the dispossession of landlords, of the destruction of all private enterprise, which in turn spells the disruption of the caste, indeed of the family system of the country. Even though on leaving Russia the idea may tumble into the depths of the Sea of Japan or into the turbulence of the Amur River, its very existence, as the caustic denunciations of Japanese generals and of others amply testify, is a menace which must be pushed far beyond the immediate contact with any Japanese-held territories.

Particularly must this be done, because it is also the inspirer of a system of labor relations which neither Japanese finance nor Japanese industry cares to tolerate. It is not for nothing that the Japanese concessionaires on the island of Sakhalin keep prodding their Foreign Office into protesting to Moscow the enforcement of Russian work hours on their enterprises. To the Russians such a protest signifies an attempt to encroach on Soviet sovereignty, the one thing on which they have never compromised even in times of greatest internal weakness and direst external peril.

The source of greatest conflict between Japanese and Russian ideology and usage stems from their respective attitudes toward other races and peoples, especially those who happen to be their immediate neighbors or live under their regime. The Russians, while exacting absolute political submission from any people or nation that is a part of the Soviet Union, do not seek to denationalize language, culture, or ways of life whenever these are not in violation of Soviet policy. Nor do the Russians withhold important offices from a minority group. On the contrary, they cater to the office-seeking urge of racial minorities, though never, I must emphasize, at the sacrifice of the Soviet idea and all that it implies.

Leaders of national minorities have been deposed and executed. But so have been leaders of the leading nationalities, such as the Russian and the Ukrainian. Some of Stalin's closest friends, Georgians and Russians, have also been executed. Again and again the Kremlin has sent Russians and others to take over the positions of deposed or executed natives. This has always happened during a purge, especially during the purge of 1936–38. But always these leaders and emissaries are required to learn the language of the minority which they are to lead or to serve. When I was in Erivan, the capital of Armenia, interviewing members of the Council of Commissars, that is of the Armenian Cabinet, I often needed the services of an interpreter because members of the council spoke Russian too imperfectly for free conversation.

Of late there has been increasing pressure, through the curriculum in the schools, for the racial minorities diligently to learn Russian, so that there would be a common medium of expression between them and Moscow and those who speak the language of Moscow. But I know of not a single instance where, within the borders of a minority, the native language has had to give precedence to the Russian as the chief language of study in the schools or of speech in Soviet institutions. Russian officials and university professors who are sent to work in the Ukraine, for example, Georgia, or in the territory of some other minority group, must learn the language of this group within a specified period of time. Not all of them do it thoroughly, especially if the language is difficult, as so many Eastern languages are. But the policy is to make them learn. Army officers in the Far East, who are stationed near or within the territory of Biro-Bidjan, the Jewish autonomous republic, have told me that they are encouraged to learn Yiddish so they may address the natives in their own language, though there is hardly a Jew there who does not understand Russian.

Despite the violences of the Soviet Revolution, despite radical changes in policy including the substitution of the Russian instead of the Latin alphabet in the newly created written languages of certain minorities, the preservation of the native tongue and native culture is not only encouraged but firmly upheld. One of the largest theaters in Moscow has specialized in presenting programs of racial minorities in their own language, their own costumes, their own tradition. The entertainers, chiefly amateurs, come from all over the far-flung Soviet lands, and so great is the demand for tickets that these are usually bought out as soon as placed on sale. The recognition that is thus accorded to the art of minorities only enhances group consciousness, group identity, and group pride.

Even in cases when a minority group living in a community of its own does not care to cultivate its own language, it has no choice in the matter. In the Crimea, for example, I visited schools on Jewish collective farms. The chief language of study was Yiddish; all the textbooks were in Yiddish. Yet during the intermissions the children and the teachers spoke only Russian. When I asked for an explanation of this seeming incongruity the students, even more than the teachers, replied that they didn't care much for the Yiddish language. They had petitioned the Soviets in Simferopol, the capital of the Crimea, for the privilege of making Russian the chief language of study. But the petition was denied on the ground that inasmuch as they were a racial minority living in their own community, they were obliged to study in their native tongue.

The case of the Buryat Mongols is especially significant and bears immediately and momentously on the conflict between Russia and Japan over the treatment of racial minorities; also, incidentally, on the unity of the Russian people in the war against Germany. I visited these people east and west of Lake Baikal. There are only about 300,000 of them and their autonomous republic borders on Outer Mongolia, with which they have much in common. In the pre-Soviet days they had been chiefly nomads wandering with their herds of cattle and horses all over the far-stretching steppes. They were living in tents or in houses with a hole in the center of the roof for the escape of smoke. They revered women, especially those capable of child-bearing, and they were superlatively kind to children. They had very few songs and very few dances of their own. They loved color and wore the brightest clothes of any people in Russia—brighter than the costumes of the Cossacks. They practiced shamanism—an ancient religion in which the shaman was more of a healer than a priest.

I lived for a week with one of the leading Buryat shamans, a man named Stepanov, a Russian name incidentally, though he claimed to be a full-blooded Buryat. He told me remarkable stories of cures he had achieved with his shamanist practices, but he admitted that he was helpless against syphilis and tuberculosis. Whenever he recognized such diseases in a patient he advised him to go to a "white man," that is to a Russian doctor. The Buryats had no schools in their own language and no alphabet except the one of ancient origin known chiefly to Buddhist lamas.

Since the coming of the Soviets, and especially since the arrival of the Five-Year Plans, the life and the condition of the Buryats have undergone a striking change. Their lands and their herds of cattle have been collectivized. Their so-called "kulaks" have suffered only less severely than those of the white people. The more impoverished the minority and the more persecuted or neglected it was in Czarist times, the more lenient has been the Soviet in the enforcement of revolutionary policy. Now, of course, Buryat kulaks have gone the way of other kulaks. But scholars have simplified the Buryat language, have composed a grammar, textbooks, a dictionary, also lawbooks for court procedure. There are 865 schools in the Buryat-Mongol Republic, 95,000 pupils, and the leading language is Buryat. In 1936 as high as 84 per cent of the population was literate in their native tongue. Ulan-Ude, the capital of the republic, boasts a teachers' institute, an agricultural college, a veterinary school, a state theater, a state opera house, in all of which Buryat Mongolian is spoken. The project for a university has gone beyond discussion and planning. The war will delay its opening. But when it does begin to function, the major language of study will be Buryat Mongolian.

The Buryat Council of Commissars, which is equivalent to a cabinet in other countries, receives instructions on basic policy from Moscow. The secretary of the Communist party and the entire Communist organizations vigilantly enforce the observance of these instructions. But the members of the council are made up largely of Buryats, and so are the officials in other Soviet positions. Once late at night I arrived in a village in which the majority of the population happened to be Russian. But the chairman of the Soviet was a Buryat young woman. Her husband was a Russian, which is demonstrative of another feature in Russian ideology and Russian character—an absence of feeling of racial superiority. Russians and natives all over Siberia freely intermarry. They did so in the old days too, even as White Russians in Manchukuo and China freely intermarry with the Chinese. The Russian has never been super-race conscious, and under the Soviet this trait has become a sanctified part of the new ideology.

In the universities of the country, in European Russia as well as Siberia, students continually intermarry.

The condition of Outer Mongolia, or of the Mongolian People's Republic, which is under complete Russian control and which has been a bloody bone of contention between Russia and Japan, is especially illuminating. Information on this closely sheltered country is more than meager. The Russians have permitted few foreigners to visit it. When I was in Ulan-Ude, capital of Buryat Mongolia, I approached Russian authorities for permission to go by the Soviet bus to Ulan Bator, the capital of Outer Mongolia. But it was never given me. Countless other writers and investigators have sought to enter the country but with no better results. The Russians themselves print almost nothing on the subject.

But the Japanese, because of their special interest in Outer Mongolia, have printed a detailed account of it in the *Far East Yearbook* (1941). This account is all the more remarkable because it comes from Japanese sources. The area of Outer Mongolia is about 1,875,000 square miles, or more than a million square miles larger than Manchukuo. The population is about 850,000, chiefly Mongols. The birth rate is low, only 0.5 per cent, because of the prevalence of disease that causes sterility. Yet, says this Japanese source, "owing to the improvement of medical facilities and the elevation of the cultural standard of the people in recent years, there has been a decrease in social diseases" which leads to an increase in the population.

The Mongolian People's Republic was founded in 1924 by a pro-Soviet faction and of course with decisive Soviet help. Prior to this time education was the almost exclusive privilege of the nobility, the officials, the lamas. Among the nomadic masses there were few who could read and write. Now there are six high schools in the country, seventy elementary schools, also special schools for the migratory nomads. Likewise there are technical institutes, medical and veterinary schools, all in the native language. There are one hundred and thirty-nine Mongol doctors and pharmacists, while seven hundred and fifty-three others are engaged in health service. There are newspapers, magazines, motion pictures, theaters, always in the Mongolian tongue.

In Ulan Bator there is a national theater and four newspapers, including one of the Red army. The writings of Joseph Stalin, H. G. Wells, Henri Barbusse, the Russian poet Pushkin, Nikolai Gogol, and Maxim Gorky have been translated into Mongolian. Gogol's *Inspector General* has been in the repertoire of the Mongolian theater. Until the coming of the People's Republic, according to the Japanese *Far East Yearbook,* there was not a single manufacturing plant in the country. Now there are machine shops, brickyards, wool-washing factories, textile mills, felt manufactories, tanneries, shops for tailoring sheepskin coats, and shoe factories that turn out 100,000 pairs of shoes a year. The seven highways in the country unite it with Russia and seven hundred trucks carry freight, while nine bus lines carry passengers and mail.

From this Japanese account of Outer Mongolia it is evident that vast progress has been made in education and in national culture—because all the institutions are in the native language—and also in elevating natives to leading political positions, though the court of last resort in everything is Moscow.

The same Japanese yearbook (1940), in discussing Manchukuo, states that out of 4,200,000 children in Manchukuo eligible for schools, only 1,800,000 can be accommodated, less than one half! "In the Manchu days," it goes on, "there were two universities in Mukden, one each in Chinchou and Kirin, and two in Harbin, which were under Soviet influence. After the Manchukuan incident [meaning Japanese occupation of Manchukuo] these institutions had to be closed due to the disturbances." There are now new middle schools and some schools of college standing in Manchukuo. But out of a teaching staff of three hundred and seventy-nine, only one hundred are Chinese, the others are Japanese, and the system of education is aiming to indoctrinate the Chinese youth with ideals of loyalty to Japan. The spirit of the education is completely Japanese, hence the preponderance of Japanese teachers in the middle schools and colleges.

Manchukuo has undergone a stupendous economic development since the coming of the Japanese. Railroads, factories, highways, mines have been developed everywhere, yet almost exclusively for the profit of Japanese. Chinese cannot even obtain permission to launch an enterprise of any significant size. They must be content with being peasants and laborers. For Japanese investors, speculators, adventurers, fortune seekers, Manchukuo has been a land of promise, though since the outbreak of the war there has been a certain amount of stagnation owing chiefly to lack of trade with Germany. The importing of German machinery and the exporting of Manchukuan soybeans to Germany have come to a standstill since the outbreak of the Russo-German war. Thus political office of importance, advancement in business, opportunity in the professions are rarely open to the Chinese. They are being pushed down with deliberate callousness into the lowest stratum of society.

During my stay in Dairen, the leading city of southern Manchuria, as I sauntered about the streets, I was impressed with the presence everywhere of Chinese laborers —street cleaners, track workers on the trolley line, longshoremen in the harbor, janitors. I discussed this feature of Chinese life with officials of the South Manchuria Railway, which is the economic as well as the political dictator of the country. These officials were pleased that I had made the observation and explained with marked pleasure that it was the policy of the Japanese to provide work for the Chinese population, more work than the Russians, who had once held the city, or the Chinese themselves could have offered the Chinese masses. I then asked if Chinese ever rose to positions of engineers or executives on the railroad, or in any of the multitudinous enterprises that the railroad was operating. The reply I got was that in some instances Chinese were entrusted with responsible offices. I asked for the number of such favored Chinese. The answer was that the information would have to be looked up and it would be sent to me. That was thirteen years ago. I am still waiting for this information.

The fact is that there are neither Chinese engineers nor Chinese executives on the South Manchuria Railway, nor in any of the Japanese institutions in southern Manchukuo.

Early in 1942 Masaharu Homma, the English-speaking Japanese general who first led the fight in Bataan against General MacArthur, appealed to the Philippine peasantry to return to their homes, resume work, and harvest the crops. An apostle of "Asia for Asiatics," he addressed the Filipinos as "brothers." On the fall of Singapore, Hideki Tojo, the Japanese Premier, in his speech before both houses of the Diet, said: "The attitude of Japan toward the people of China is that of regarding them as our brothers."

The use of the word "brother" reveals the Japanese as infinitely more astute propagandists than the Germans. Unlike the Nazis, the Japanese do not scream their racial superiority to the peoples they conquer. They say just the opposite. They seek to flatter these people into confidence in Japanese integrity and good will. But their aim is the same as that of the Germans—the assertion of their own superiority and the complete exploitation and degradation of conquered peoples. They are the masters, and they never tarry long to assert their mastery, with methods no less arbitrary than those the Germans have perfected and no less brutal when they encounter active opposition.

The case of Korea is even more enlightening. Annexed in 1910, Korea has a population of over twenty-one millions. There the policy of denationalization has been gaining continuous momentum. In 1939 the governor general outlawed the Korean language in official business, even in the homes of those Koreans who happen to hold government office, which is always of low rank. Of course such a law is not easy to enforce, but it is demonstrative of the utter lack of regard for the language or the culture of the Koreans. In Seoul, the capital of Korea, there were in the year 1940 only two newspapers, one in the Korean language. This was a concession to those Koreans who either wouldn't or couldn't read Japanese. But the primary function of this newspaper is to propagate Japanese-inspired ideas and ideals. There are no schools in the Korean language and Korean teachers must vow allegiance to Japan. In 1940 there were only one hundred and eight secondary schools. Though annually about one thousand boys and girls apply for admission, no more than one hundred and fifty are admitted. Cities, villages, mountains, and rivers have been given Japanese names, precisely as the Germans in Posen and in Czechoslovakia have substituted German for Polish or Czech names. Since 1939 Korean children who fail to bear Japanese names are barred from schools altogether. Censorship is so rigid that there is no Korean literature.

In the economic sphere the highest and best positions are held by Japanese. Though 77 per cent of the population is peasant, about half of them are tenant farmers or hired hands. Though Korea is noted for its rice, most of the white rice goes to Japan. Koreans must content themselves chiefly with a mixture of rice and barley. In business, because of superior credit opportunities and of political support from the governor general, Japanese are in a favored position. More often than not they smother the aspiring Korean businessman the moment he seeks to compete with them.

In a basic sense Japan—the Prussia of Asia—is pursuing the same ends in Asia that the Germans have already achieved in western and central Europe. They are the master race, the master nation, and arrogate to themselves the control over finance, politics, education, industry, agriculture—everything that relates to power and profits. They are infinitely more tactful than Germans, except when actively opposed. They are the overlords of everything. No wonder that the late Rabindranath Tagore, the eminent poet of India, felt constrained to say:

"All Asia once admired Japan and cherished great hopes that Asia had at last found in Japan the answer to the West. . . . But Japan betrayed the awakening hope . . . represents an even worse menace to the defenseless peoples of the East . . . worse than its economic exploitation are the massacres which it perpetrates day after day and its shameless defense of inhumanity."

The recent meeting between Chiang Kai-shek and Gandhi is a direct answer to Japan's determined attempt to impose herself on the people of Asia with no more regard or reverence for their national sentiments than Germany is showing for the people she has conquered in Europe.

Clearly there is no compromise between the racial and the national equality which Russia, a white nation, advocates and practices in Asia, and the racial or national inequality which Japan continually imposes on other peoples. In a world made tempestuously aware of racial and national identity this is an issue of explosive consequence all over Asia. Their own attitude the Japanese have no wish to change. Russia's they have no way of changing. True enough Sovietism implies policies and practices which Asiatic peoples might never care to accept, against which they might battle with all their energy. But the proclamation and the enforcement of racial and national equality at a time when Japan imposes shattering inferiority are forces the Japanese must reckon with. All the more galling to the Japanese is this aspect of Russian ideology because Russia borders on Korea, Manchukuo, and, through Outer Mongolia, also reaches, however indirectly, Inner Mongolia, thus only heightening the disaffection of these peoples. For this reason too there is nothing the Japanese would like better than to push Russia beyond the possibility of contact or influence, however remote, with their conquered peoples.

Outer Mongolia only adds fuel to the conflict over racial minorities and territorial aspirations. Soviet-controlled, it is directly in the way of Japanese expansion on the Asiatic mainland. Japan has been seeking to wrench it from Soviet influence so it could unite it with Inner Mongolia, consolidate its territorial and strategic position, and thus obtain a good base from which to attack Siberia. This is precisely what the Russians have been striving to prevent. Japan's seizure of Outer Mongolia would expose about nine hundred miles of the trans-Siberian railway to

Japanese onslaught. It would bring a Japanese army on the border of one of the richest and most livable parts of Siberia. It would make Russia's defense of her Asiatic lands infinitely more difficult. That is why in 1921 the Soviets, without annexing Outer Mongolia, had assumed a decisive part in the direction of its daily life and its international relations. One of the first and most popular motion pictures the gifted Soviet director Pudovkin made— *Storm over Asia*—is laid in Outer Mongolia and gives a vivid and sympathetic portrayal of the people there.

Recently the Russians built a railroad from Ulan-Ude, the capital of Buryat Mongolia, to Kyakhta, on the border of Outer Mongolia. The purpose of this railroad is obvious. As already narrated, the trade, the education, above all the military defense of the country are under Russian supervision and control. Again and again Japan has sought to establish diplomatic residence in Outer Mongolia, but to no avail. Again and again Japan has attempted to force her way into Outer Mongolia. Invariably the onslaughts were shattered by an array of military power which lacked none of the modern weapons of warfare. Russia is always on hand to thwart Japanese attempts to foist themselves on Outer Mongolia as they have on Manchukuo and on Inner Mongolia. Russia will fight for Outer Mongolia as she will for Vladivostok, for Sakhalin, for Kamchatka. None other than Stalin has said as much.

With Outer Mongolia in Russian hands, with a powerful army guarding its borders, a still more powerful army in Siberia ready to rush to its defense, the invasion of

Siberia by Japan is more than hampered. Meanwhile, Soviet invasion of Manchukuo and Inner Mongolia is made more easy. Not that Moscow has evinced any wish to make such an invasion, but Japanese generals must think of it. Were Japan attempting to seize Vladivostok or Sakhalin or any Russian outpost in the Far East, Soviet armies would most assuredly attempt a thrust into Manchukuo and Inner Mongolia. Thus Outer Mongolia alone is a source of endless diplomatic battling and border fighting between Japan and Russia.

Russia's relations with China are another thorn in the side of Japan's imperialism. In the early twenties the late Sun Yat-sen invited the Russians to come to China and aid in organizing the campaign against foreign domination. Gladly Russia responded. Moscow sent General Galen, alias General Blukher, one of her most brilliant soldiers, to Canton. Moscow also sent one of her shrewdest political propagandists, Michael Borodin. Blukher and his assistants organized the Whampoa military academy in Canton. Borodin organized propaganda. In 1927, with the triumph of the Chinese Nationalist armies in Shanghai, Chiang Kai-shek broke with the Russians. Mercilessly he put to death Chinese and Russian Communists whenever he could lay his hands on them. Russia and China became bitter enemies.

In 1937, with the Japanese invasion of China, they became friends again. Russia signed a non-aggression pact with China, and to help the Chinese armies, imposed an embargo on trade with Japan. On September 21, 1937, in

Geneva before the Assembly of the League of Nations, Litvinov, then Commissar for Foreign Affairs in Moscow, denounced Japanese aggression. "On the Asiatic continent," he said, "one state without a declaration of war, without occasion or excuse whatever, falls upon another. China floods it with armies one hundred strong, blockades coasts, paralyzes trade in one of the great centers of world commerce (Shanghai)." Russia did more. She extended credit to China, shipped ammunition, and flew aviators, military advisers, organizers to the Chinese battle front. With Japanese occupation of the coastal cities and harbors, Russian help became all the more imperative. Russian engineers, with the help of Chinese labor, built highways over deserts and mountains for the transport of ammunition. Openly and energetically, Russia came to China's assistance.

The Japanese protested. They intensified border clashes with Russian armies. They were seeking a weak link in the Russian defense lines with a view to involving Russia in so much fighting that help to China would be stopped. The Russians struck back with diplomacy and gunfire. Since the clash on the Amur River in 1937, they have never permitted Japan to win a military victory and have never acquiesced in any of her territorial demands.

The establishment of the Jewish Autonomous Territory of Birobidjan can only be regarded by Japanese imperialists as one more Soviet provocation. In some measure Birobidjan may even be responsible for the vogue of anti-Semitism that is sweeping Japan.

In 1928 the Soviets opened this territory of 14,200 square miles in the Far East to Jewish colonization. The country is primitive but abounds in agricultural and mineral resources. Soviet Jews do not particularly care to migrate there. Most of them, especially young people, have no desire to build up a separate Jewish colony in Russia. Jews from other parts of Europe would gladly go there were the opportunity open to them and were transportation available. Though the territory is twice the size of Palestine, the total population is as yet no more than 70,000. But it is rapidly becoming industrialized. Since it is located in the bend of the Amur River, the Japanese are growing apprehensive. They do not relish the thought of an energetic people like the Jews settling a land on the border of Manchukuo, thereby adding to the economic and military strength of Russia. The Japanese must be particularly irked by the Soviet project to erect a steel plant in Birobidjan. Yet they cannot stop the Birobidjan enterprise unless they make war on Russia.

Meanwhile, they have embarked on a campaign of anti-Semitism which in the virulence of its language is comparable to that of Nazi Germany. All the more extraordinary is this campaign because the Japanese know hardly anything about Jews. The few Jews who settled in Japan in the sixteenth century have long since been absorbed and assimilated. There has been no Jewish migration to Japan. Jews are represented neither in finance, industry, the arts, politics, nor in the professions. None of the leading financial magnates are Jewish. There is no so-called

Jewish influence anywhere. Yet *Asahi,* mouthpiece of the Japanese army, charges that Jews "have re-elected Roosevelt for a third term and had coaxed Churchill to wage war against Germany; the Jews also backed Stalin; the Jews are conspiring to overthrow the world's ruling powers." German inspiration is only too obvious in this outburst of hate.

Yet none of the clashes already discussed must stir Japanese apprehension as much as the development of Siberia. However heavy the dynamite that already loads the relations between Japan and Russia—economic, political, international, racial—heavier still and more explosive is the conflict over Siberia, the vast and powerful new empire that Russia is creating at the very doorstep of Japan.

CHAPTER VIII

The Siberian Legend

LEGENDS DIE HARD, and no legend is so slow in dying as that of Siberia. To this day the non-Russian world thinks of it as a bleak wilderness, with tragedy and death stalking its immense spaces, with neither cheer nor hope relieving its vast desolation. George Kennan's dramatic volumes on *Siberia and the Exile System,* published in 1891 and. depicting the life and the lot of political exiles, and Dostoievski's *Memoirs of a Dead House,* portraying in fiction his own torment in Siberian jails during the four years of his incarceration, have made an imperishable impression on the world, particularly on the English-speaking countries; for people in America and in England still almost shudder at the mention of the word "Siberia."

Yet Siberia now is saving Russia. Were it not for Siberia and all that it is and contains, in resources, in industries, in space,. in climate, the Red armies could hardly have withstood the poundings of the Reichswehr in the first five months of fighting. It is because of Siberia that Russia, in this writer's judgment, is utterly unconquerable, even when she fights simultaneously against Japan and Germany. Its size alone—interminable forests, mountain ranges, swamps, together with its mighty rivers, which flow north into the Arctic waters—offers unrivaled positions for defense and concealment. If driven off the main arteries of transportation, armies can withdraw into the wilderness, bide their time, then sally forth when least expected and strike at the enemy, especially now when all Siberia is rapidly becoming a gigantic machine shop.

Czarist Siberia was one thing; Soviet Siberia is quite another. Still a center of political exiles, Siberia is Russia's wonderland. At present it is the greatest boom land in the world. There is nothing anywhere comparable to the stupendous development in that vast and little-known continent. It literally roars and flames with effort from one end to the other. When the war between Russia and Japan breaks out, two Russias will be fighting—European Russia and Siberia. Both will be under the same sovereignty, both will be Soviet, both will be governed from Moscow, but each will have its own armies, its own supply depots, its own general staff, and will fight in its own way. Long ago the Russians worked out plans to make European Russia and Siberia militarily independent of one another, so that in the event of war in both parts, each can fight independently of the other.

At present Siberia, including the Urals, is the most industrialized part of the Asiatic mainland. With scores, indeed with hundreds of plants from the fighting zones being newly set up on its far-stretching lands, and hundreds more in process of construction, it is becoming more and more so all the time. In no other one land in Asia are there so many gigantic steel plants and all manner of machine shops. Siberia and the Urals manufacture at least as much steel as does all Japan, and what Siberia now has is only a beginning of what is to come, of what already exists in the blueprints of the Soviets.

In 1939 there were about twenty million people in Siberia. But the migration there has only begun and its numbers are mounting rapidly. In size Siberia is about as large as the United States and European Russia together, and according to professors of the University of Irkutsk, with whom I once discussed the subject, someday Siberia will boast as large a population as either the United States or European Russia now have, perhaps larger. Only in parts is it encompassed by a severe climate, too severe for extensive colonization. But it abounds in resources, which, when developed, can support about eight or ten times its present population. The prospect of such a population even in the faraway and unpredictable future must stir more than the apprehension of the Japanese militarist. He must prevent it by all means at his disposal or run the risk of finding himself and his grandiose ambitions for a Japan-ruled Asia pushed back, perhaps off the mainland of the continent. He must act soon and decisively, and fortify his hold of Asia, for with the vast and powerful

Soviet empire in Siberia growing like a well-watered plant, he may never again have the chance.

When I boarded the trans-Siberian express for my first journey to Siberia, I couldn't help thinking of all that I had read and heard of the country. Vividly I remembered Nekrasov's poem, "Russian Women," parts of which I had learned by heart while a student in a Russian public school. This is a poem over which several generations not only of children but of literate adults have mourned and wept. It is the story of the so-called Decembrist women, the wives of the leaders of the Decembrist Revolution of 1825, who forsook their luxurious homes in the capital of the Czars and journeyed on horse and sledge to the far-away places of exile to which their husbands had been sent by the frightened and enraged Nicholas I. What a desolate and anguished land Siberia is in that memorable poem by one of Russia's most beloved poets!

Yet the closer the train on which I traveled drew to the Urals, the less I thought of Nekrasov's Siberia, particularly as the companions in my compartment were engineers who were on their way to construction assignments in the Baikal country. One of them was Siberian born, and he spoke of his native land with as fervid a boastfulness as native Californians speak of their state. To him Siberia was the one land of promise in the world, the hope of Russia, of all Asia, indeed of all mankind, for the Siberian was not only physically the pick of humanity in all Russia, but was bound by neither tradition nor fear nor the petty-mindedness of Europeans. The son of a rebel, or a pioneer, or an ordinary criminal, the Siberian, the engineer, raced on, had fire in his blood, steel in his bones, and all the audacity in the world in his soul. He understood the forest, the steppe, the wild beast, and now that he had gotten his "revolutionary freedom," he would show Moscow, yes, and New York, what he could do in building up a new empire and a new civilization. Cities, factories, farms, cows, wheat—Siberia would have the best of everything and the most too. Did I ever taste Krasnoyarsk honey? Ah, there was honey as smooth to the tongue as it was fragrant to the nostrils, and, once eaten, no other honey will ever again taste like honey. Never, for there are not flowers and blossoms like those in Krasnoyarsk, and no forests either. Ah, what a land, what a treasure, what a glory was this vast and noble and limitless Siberia!

On and on he talked, with ever-heightening fervor. This is the way other natives of Siberia speak, many of them. They do not even like to call themselves Russians. They are *Sibiriaks*—a people apart, with gifts, virtues, a destiny all their own, the most grandiose of any people in the world. And didn't I know that in the early sixties Siberians plotted to break away from the Czar and to make the American Constitution the fundamental law of the land? Yes, they did! . . . Looking out of the window, the words that tumbled out of the man's eloquent lips assumed a clearer and richer meaning. Fields and meadows, trees and lakes, flowers and grains, cattle and horses, and brilliant sunshine beckoned from every direction.

The railroad stations were depressing. Crowds everywhere, on the floor, on doorsteps, around the railroad tracks; women with suckling babes; men sleeping and snoring on the bare floor; mothers picking lice out of their children's heads; pickpockets snuggling close to a well-dressed person with the hope of snatching a pocketbook, a costly shawl, a basketful of food; beggars too; the blind, the lame, the halt, making the sign of the cross over their bodies, bowing low and holding out a rough and dirty hand for a kopeck, a *grivna* (ten-kopeck piece), a slice of bread, "for Christ's sake"; smells, cries, and all kinds of noises.

Sauntering around the railroad stations, rude and not always well kept, one would get the impression that Siberia was a land of unredeemable ruin and poverty, which is precisely what foreign travelers often say it is. Being, of course, a pioneer country, people swarm there in search of improvement or else are exiles from cities and villages in European Russia, all waiting for trains, waiting and waiting, for there never are enough trains to accommodate the crowds that want to ride in them, to new regions, thousands of miles away from their old homes. . . . Waiting passengers in Siberian railroad stations make one feel as though humanity in Siberia is always on the move, always leaving an unfinished home, always thinking it can build a better one elsewhere.

Siberia is rich in the things that make for life and progress. Its wealth in minerals has as yet been barely catalogued: gold and platinum, among the most abundant deposits in the world; coal and iron; silver and copper; lead and manganese; mercury and zinc; tin and potash; oil too, already in process of exploitation, and being further explored; lead and bauxite.

Then there are the interminable forests—with much of them still unexplored, with the richest reserves of fur in the world: bear and squirrel; black fox, silver fox, polar fox; ermine and sable; polecat and lynx; badger and beaver; weasel and wild goat, and of course deer, especially reindeer—vast herds wandering in the tundras of the north and supplying meat for the army and for the factory districts. In all there are one hundred and fifty species of animals in Siberia whose furs are commercially valuable.

There are tens of thousands of men in Siberia who live only by hunting; that is, in winter they lose themselves in the interminable forests and gather vast amounts of pelts. When they come out in the spring, they sell their furs and loaf, imbibing heavily and squandering their rich earnings. With labor needed everywhere, in the factory and on the land, strenuous efforts are being made to tame these hardy adventurers and make their summers as productive as their winters. But the older men, like the beasts they hunt, are beyond the discipline, and when they face the danger of compulsory labor or of too much propaganda on the wastefulness of their lives, they flee to the wilderness and remain there safe from official scrutiny, from the observance of all men, until such time as they feel lonely again and in need of concourse with human beings, or only of the vodka that they must drink to keep up their spirits or their faith in themselves and in their odd way of life.

On reaching Sverdlovsk, the capital of Siberia, I found it swarming with young people, hatless or with caps on their heads, brief cases under their arms, running from office to office, precisely as in Moscow. The city heaved with action: new buildings going up, old buildings coming down or undergoing a process of enlargement. The machine age was clanging away, without letup, all day long. In the evenings the park was thronged with workers, startlingly young and better dressed than young people in Moscow. The band played without letup precisely as the machine during the day clanged. The winding paths and roadways resounded with loud talk and playful capers. Here was youth at its best—hearty, mirthful, boisterously self-confident.

In the immense square almost directly opposite the old cathedral stood the gabled house of the engineer Yepatyev, a historic house now. It was there that the last of the Romanovs, who had ruled Russia for three hundred and one years, spent his last days. It was in the basement of this house that late one night the Czar and his family were executed. A strange, historic coincidence—that the first Romanov should have come out of a monastery named Yepatyev and that the last should meet his death in a house that had been owned by a man named Yepatyev.

I wanted to visit the house and see the basement in which one of the great imperial dynasties of the world was brought to a sudden end. But no one in authority would grant the necessary permission and the caretaker, in spite of all my importuning, would not, on his own responsibility, accommodate me. Finally, in a small office, I came on a man who had participated in the execution of the Romanov family. Frankly he explained that ordinarily, as a matter of Soviet hospitality to a foreign visitor, he would gladly accord me the privilege of visiting the Yepatyev house. But I was a writer, and that made a difference. People in Sverdlovsk, as all over the Soviet Union, no longer cared to discuss the Czar in life or in death or to help foreign writers discuss him in the foreign press. Still, as long as I was in the city he would not withhold from me the opportunity of seeing the house. Then as I was leaving he counseled me to bother less about people and institutions that were dead beyond resurrection and more about people and institutions that were making the Urals and Siberia a new world—a world of steel and engines, of schools and universities. . . .

I often thought of this man as I wandered on in the Urals and in Siberia. His words were no empty boast or idle dream, for the Urals and Siberia, despite outward uncouthness, have become a land of steel and engines, of schools and universities.

CHAPTER IX

The Triumphs of Siberia—in the Factory

In THE summer of 1929 I was on a boat with a party of American engineers who were on their way to the Urals to build the first modern steel plant there. The decision to erect this plant was made in Moscow on January 16, 1929. In March, even before the American engineers arrived, the work had started. For three years it went on without interruption amid hunger and disease, pain and sweat, with workers living in barracks, in tents, with neither enough winter clothing nor winter covering to keep them comfortable in the months of blasting cold, with neither enough doctors nor hospitals to care for the sick. The land was steppe, bare of forest but rich in highest quality iron ore, mountains of it, and within easy reach of limestone, dolomite, fireproof clay, molding sand, other necessary accessories, all but coal. The nearest coal at that time was twelve hundred and fifty miles away, deep in the heart of Siberia, in Kusnetsk, which boasts two thirds of the coal deposits hitherto discovered in all Russia. Soon afterward a steel plant was started in Kusnetsk and trains kept rolling from Kusnetsk to Magnitogorsk and back again, carrying ore to the one and bringing coal to the other.

On February 1, 1932, the first pig iron of Magnitogorsk flowed out of a modern blast furnace, the first of its kind in Asiatic Russia, or east of the Ukraine. Since then the steel mills of Kusnetsk and Magnitogorsk have become the pride of Siberia, the rock on which its stupendous industrial superstructure is being reared. Since then also increasing deposits of iron have been uncovered in or near Kusnetsk and increasing amounts of coal have been dug in the Urals and in Karaganda, which is only half the distance from Magnitogorsk that Kusnetsk is.

Neither of these gigantic steel plants confines itself solely to the manufacture of steel. The territory all around is dotted with chimney stacks—foundries, brick yards, chemical shops, power plants, all manner of manufacturing establishments that supply accessories to the steel plants or convert steel into finished products, now principally munitions. In time, when the new additions are completed, Magnitogorsk and Kusnetsk will be among the foremost steel plants not only in Asia—that they now are—but in the world.

The Urals are a small strip of land from thirty-one to ninety-three miles wide, 1,550 miles long, running from the polar sea to the summer-parched desert. The region is literally spattered with factories, among the newest and largest on this earth. There are two reasons for the extraordinary industrial development of the Urals. First, they abound in natural wealth—iron ore, manganese, cobalt, arsenic, gold, platinum, oil, asbestos, nickel, phosphorites, potassium salt, chromites, and other highly valuable raw materials. Second, situated at the dividing line between Europe and Asia, the Urals are far removed not only from possible enemy infantry, cavalry, tanks, but also from enemy bombers, from the west as well as from the east. It is one of the most highly sheltered industrial regions in the world.

The Ural Mountains are not very high. At the point where the trans-Siberian passes they are no more than gently rolling hills. A story that I heard on the train from a Russian traveler bears significantly on this point. An American woman was traveling from China to Europe on the trans-Siberian. After more than a week of monotonous travel from Vladivostok, she was eager for a glimpse of the Ural Mountains and kept asking the conductor when the train would be passing them. With habitual Russian nonchalance the conductor kept replying: "seichas"— which literally means this hour, but figuratively may mean an eternity. The woman kept looking out of the window, thrilled at the prospect of a sight of mountains. Finally her patience came to an end and once more she said to the conductor: "When *are* we coming to the Ural Mountains?" With a show of perturbation the conductor replied, "We have just passed them, lady!" "Out of disappointment," the Russian concluded the story, "the woman flew into her compartment and stayed there until the train arrived in Moscow." Profuse and amusing are the stories that Russians love to tell about the Urals.

Up north, toward the Arctic Circle, and down south the mountains ascend to about six thousand feet. But in the central region, at Sverdlovsk, they seldom rise to a thousand feet. They are rich in minerals. Mountains Vysokaya and Blagodat at Tagil in the north and Mount Magnitnaya in the south are packed with one of the richest grades of iron ore in the world. At the very base of Magnitnaya is the new city of Magnitogorsk. Mount Vysokaya, Lebyazhya, and Blagodat, as well as the Tagil-Kushva deposits, furnish ore for one of the newest steel plants in the Urals, in Novy Tagil, and one of the most highly mechanized in the world. This plant was finished in May 1940, and only the expectation of war prevented Russia from fittingly signalizing the event as another national triumph.

In this plant manual labor will be reduced to a minimum. All manner of automatic equipment has been installed to mechanize the processes of labor. The blast furnaces are among the largest in the world. The power plant, the coke chemical plant, the rolling mills, the blooming mills, the cement shops, the other manufacturing departments are likewise completely modernized.

When completed this mill will turn out two million tons of steel a year and only a half million less tons of rolled steel. It will furnish steel and iron for one of the largest freight and passenger car shops in the world.

To the northwest of Novy Tagil is the town of Chusovaya on the rocky bank of a river by the same name. Here is the largest charcoal blast furnace in the world, also completely mechanized. It was here too that the first oil in the Urals was found. All around in the old days were manufacturing plants, about fifty of them, small in size and primitive in equipment. Now they have been rebuilt, knitted more closely together, and for the most part completely modernized.

To the west of Chusovaya lies the city of Perm, on the banks of another river, the Kama, with large shipbuilding, woodworking, engineering plants. To the east of Chusovaya and almost as far north is the city Krasno-Uralsk, with up-to-date copper smelters. Here are other cities that only a bare ten or fifteen years ago were too small to figure prominently in the industrial life of the country— Strelki, Kizel, Nizhne Tagil, Solikamsk, Berezniki, Vishera, Alapayevsk, and many others. All are booming especially now, when every available plant is turning its energies to the manufacture of armaments. Much of the ammunition used on the European front comes from these cities and factories.

In the central part of the Urals lie two of its most famous cities, Sverdlovsk and Cheliabinsk, both old, both with a rich history, both among the most gigantic industrial centers of the Soviet Union. Sverdlovsk and its far-flung suburbs are almost a continuous network of shops and factories. The machine shops, or machines to produce machines, as the Russians speak of them, are equipped with the most modern lathes and planers, the very best that American industry produces, for most of them came from America or were modeled after American models.

The word.Cheliabinsk comes from the Bashkerian word *cheliaba,* which means a hole and refers to the pools of mud in its one-time streets and roads. The groves of birch make an impressive setting for this city of sixty-horse-power caterpillar tractors and of the mightiest tanks that the Soviets are making. Every child in Russia has heard of it, especially in the villages, for there is scarcely a collective farm whose fields have not been plowed in part by the Cheliabinsk tractors. The city has its own power stations and water system. It operates electro-metallurgical shops, zinc works, and gets its coal from near-by mines and its steel from Magnitogorsk, which is not far away, and from the vicinity of Zlatoust.

Ufa is another historic city in this section of Russia. At one time it was often enough a hiding place for revolutionaries who broke away from their guards while on their march to Siberian exile. Now it is the home of oil refineries and the largest Diesel engine factory in Russia.

In a book like this it is impossible to go into lengthy and detailed descriptions of the Ural industries. Yet it is well to emphasize that since the loss of the industries in the Ukraine during the first five months of the Russo-German war, the Urals have practically become the heart of Russia's industrial system. No one outside of Russia has the remotest conception of the new factories that are being built there and that make possible the continued manufacture of armaments for the fighting armies.

It is well also to point out here that the industrial empire of the Urals would have been impossible without the services of American engineers and the purchases of American machinery. Indeed, had it not been for the inventiveness of capitalist America all along the line of industrial organization, neither European Russia nor the Urals, nor Siberia, would have been the industrial lands that they now are. The sweep and the might of the American machine shop and of the so-called Detroit assembly line, as much as any other circumstance, are responsible for the miraculous industrial transformation that the three Five-Year Plans have achieved in Russia.

Beyond the Urals eastward, all the way to the Pacific Ocean and northward to the Arctic region, stretch more machine-building factories, more steel shops, more aviation plants, more railroads, highways, air lines, and the Arctic Ocean with its new and highly sheltered passageway from Europe to Asia.

Here is Novosibirsk, the Chicago of Siberia, so-called because of its location in the midst of a rich and ever-growing agricultural and industrial region. In the old days Novosibirsk was a provincial town, with most of the houses built of logs, with most of the streets unpaved, with pigs strutting and rooting in the streets and cattle lying in the courtyards. It was chiefly a trading center for the disposal of grain, butter, livestock, and other agricultural products. It had comparatively little industry—a cotton mill, a sawmill, a creamery, a tannery, and many of the artisan shops for which old Russia was justly famous. In 1917 its population was only 69,800. It had neither a water nor a sewerage system. It had several schools whose academic standing, as was the case with so many of the schools in the old days, was excellent. Yet more than half of the population was illiterate. It was a town of taverns, and a symbol of the age of wood that obtained in Siberia even more than in European Russia.

Now Novosibirsk is one of the fastest-growing cities in Asia and in the world. As I walked along its many new streets, wide and bright from the whiteness of its newly built and towering brick buildings, I felt as though I was somewhere in America's Middle West, in a boom town. The city swarmed with more people than it could properly care for, and more and more newcomers from all over the land were constantly arriving. At present the population of Novosibirsk must be over half a million, and with the fresh, ever-swelling tide of migration to Siberia, it would be foolhardy even to attempt to make a forecast of its growth in the near future.

In winter the climate is severe enough, the cold going down to 60 degrees below zero. In summer in the daytime the heat may rise to over 100 degrees Fahrenheit. The nights are cool. There are forests and wheat lands all around the far-stretching territory. Factories are continually on the ascendancy. Between 1931 and 1937 no less than forty large industrial establishments have been built.

Here is a plant that manufactures machinery for the gold mines of Siberia; still another, one of the largest in the world, for the manufacture of agricultural implements for the immense Siberian grain farms. Shoes, textiles, furniture, soap, bricks are among the leading industries. So is meat packing. There is a water system, a sewerage system in the city, a new opera house with a seating capacity of over 2,000 and a smaller hall in the same building for concerts with a seating capacity of 800. Here is the largest railway engineering college in Russia, a medical school, and one of the largest railway stations anywhere, with a capacity of 4,000 passengers daily. In 1938 there were ten technical schools in the city, a conservatory of music, a dramatic school, an institute for the training of physical-culture teachers, seven schools of university rank, including the medical school. Here is a new hospital built in the heart of a pine wood. It is a part of the medical school and is a station for blood transfusion. Here are also motion-picture houses, over two hundred libraries, clinics, dispensaries, scattered all over the far-flung city and its outlying suburbs.

Despite its many factories, skyscrapers, busses and trolleys, Novosibirsk, like all new industrial cities in Russia, especially in Asia, gives one the impression of roughness and feverishness, of action and more action, with scarcely a trace of the contemplation and the heart searching which have made the old Russian literature so great and which were so distinctive a feature of the life of the pre-revolutionary Russian gentry and the intelligentsia. There is as yet little physical comfort for the people. The hotels are always so overcrowded that without the help of the local Soviet I never should have found a room. The only way the hotel could accommodate me was to induce two Russian guests to sleep in another room which was more like a dormitory, so crowded was it with cots and beds. There is nothing beautiful or fashionable about Novosibirsk, hardly a vestige of luxury, much overcrowding, much arguing—now and then Russian temper snaps—also fist fights. Yet there is much gayety, especially in the parks, and above all immeasurable faith in the destiny and the future of Novosibirsk and all Siberia. It is an old city that has been made young by youth and enterprise.

Not far from Novosibirsk is the city of Barnaul. In 1926 it had a population of 73,858 and at the time the census was taken in 1939 it had leaped to 148,129. The rapid, almost geometric increase in population is an outstanding feature of all new and all old cities in Siberia and in other parts of Russian Asia. Barnaul is situated in the heart of one of the richest agricultural sections of Siberia and is the seat of one of the largest textile *combinats* in the world. Raw cotton and wool keep traveling from shop to shop, floor to floor, until the finished cloth rolls off the weaving machines.

Beyond Novosibirsk, two hundred miles eastward, is Kusnetsk, scarcely more than a village in the old days, now the home of a modern steel mill, the hub of an ever-expanding factory system, with inexhaustible reserves of coal almost at the doorstep of the blast furnaces, with all the timber in the world, with more and more iron near by, and with countless other raw materials for the manufacture of tools, automobiles, planes, and armaments.

Beyond Kusnetsk is Petrovsk, hardly ever mentioned in foreign news, bringing the age of steel to the Baikal region, with a modern mill already built and a modern city in the making. And further on, Komsomolsk, a city of youth, built by youth, run by youth, and dedicated to the manufacture of steel and to things that can be made from steel, particularly weapons of war. Below Kusnetsk, within a fold of the Amur River, is Birobidjan, still thinly populated but replete with industrial promise, with a steel mill soon to be built.

Steel plants are strung along the entire length and much of the breadth of Siberia on sites difficult to hit from the air, indeed easily concealed from the view of the pilot. The more steel Siberia makes, the more shells and projectiles, guns and tanks, fighters and bombers are available for its protection; also the more railroads, highways, airdromes to facilitate the work of such protection.

On the train on which I journeyed from Novosibirsk to Irkutsk no passengers were so intent on gazing out of the windows of the train, on studying Russian pamphlets and maps of Siberia, as was a group of Japanese students and diplomats. But they wouldn't discuss Siberia with other passengers.

To man the new factories, new population is flowing to Siberia—by plane, by train, by bus, by motor truck, by ship, and off the main highways in mile-long caravans of

wagons drawn by the little, tireless, good-natured Mongolian horses. It will flow in increasing waves, because of
the decree forbidding the millions of evacuées from the
fighting zones to return to their homes, even after these
have been reconquered. It is a sight to watch one of these
caravans rolling along, like a monumental wave, over the
Siberian land. At night the caravan stops for rest. The
horses need to be pastured; food has to be cooked; the
children must be put to sleep. Log fires light up the fields
and the woods; someone plays the inevitable accordion;
someone sings; someone scolds a wife or a husband; someone wanders off with a gun to shoot game or to fight off
skulking bandits.

Between 1926 and 1939 more than three million people
migrated to Siberia, chiefly young people, for only such
are encouraged to go, excepting, of course, those who
have no choice—the political exiles. Siberia needs not only
youth but men who know how to fight and are ready to
shoulder a rifle at an instant's notice. Komsomolsk, for
example, the steel city in the Far East, was settled by
volunteers thirty years of age and younger. At first most
of the volunteers were young men. They came by the
trainload from all over the country. They set to work
clearing the wilderness for the new city and new factories
they were to build. They divided into colonies and fended
for themselves as best they could. Then they called for
girls to join them, so they could get married and settle
down. Thousands of girls heeded the call. The pioneering
spirit is strong in the Russian, especially in the young

people, and they readily go everywhere, as their elders would not, to start new experiments and new economic developments.

Now Komsomolsk is a busy and thriving city and rearing an ever-growing young generation. Indeed it is a roaring ammunition plant and one of the mighty military fortresses in Russia's Far East.

With the influx of fresh millions to Siberia, new cities like Komsomolsk are destined to rise all over the country. Old cities, like Irkutsk, Chita, Novosibirsk, Tomsk, Omsk, Krasnoyarsk, and others are destined to push far out of their present boundaries and make of Siberia a land of metropolitan centers no less populous and no less livable than any in European Russia.

It is a far cry from the forge which Genghis Khan had brought to Siberia, some seven hundred years ago, to the gigantic steel factories that now span the country. Just as the forge was for a long time the symbol of Siberia's backwardness so the blast furnace is now the symbol of its industrial might. There is good reason to assume that the steel and iron output of Siberia is at least as large as that of Japan, though no comparative and reliable figures are now available. Oil, too, has been found in increasing quantities. Cambrian rock is soaked with it, and there are literally tens of thousands of square miles of such rock in Siberia. The discovery and exploitation of oil from cambrian rock are recent. Yet together with the other sources of oil in Siberia, in the Urals, and east of the Volga, Russia obtained in 1938 no less than five and a half million tons of oil, which is more than Germany is obtaining in all her synthetic plants.

The rise of a new and growing steel civilization in Siberia is one of the basic sources of conflict between Japan and Russia.

CHAPTER X

The Triumphs of Siberia—on the Land

In 1896, when the Soviet Revolution was no more than an idea in the minds of exiled intellectuals, or a hope of isolated and whispering factory workers and peasants, a group of Danish dairy experts were invited to Siberia to introduce the advanced methods of butter-making for which their native land was famous. Within a decade Siberian butter was known and renowned in the leading countries of Europe. In 1909 a trainload of refrigerator cars loaded with butter thundered daily toward the Baltic seaboard. From there the butter was shipped to Paris, to London, to other parts of Europe.

Siberia has always been noted for its dairies, its wheat lands, its honey, its pastures, its meadows, its flowers, which in summer grow in profusion at every hand. Its black soils are rich and extend for an enormous area. That was why so many peasants in European Russia had in the old days migrated there—peasants from the Ukraine, from White Russia, from the central regions, where, with the increase of population, the individual inheritance of land was becoming smaller and smaller. In the pre-revolutionary days there was poverty among Siberian peasants, especially among new settlers or those who had no horse of their own. But seldom did it approach the condition of sordidness that abounded in the crowded farming districts of European Russia. All along the highway from Irkutsk to Ust-Kut, as the mail bus on which I traveled passed from village to village, the sight that impressed me most was the quality of the houses. Nowhere in European Russia had I seen such uniformly large houses with such high windows and with so many decorations on doors and windows of twigs and flowers.

On the way back from Ust-Kut I stopped in the village of Ust-Urda. The bus arrived late in the night, and the inn was not much of a hostelry. Guests slept on the bare board floor in the large living room unless they brought along their own bedding. The only accommodation I was offered was floor space between two bearded and snoring men. But the food in this inn was a revelation, and how Siberians can eat! Lack of appetite is not an affliction from which Russians suffer unless they are sick, and even then food is the one thing they refuse to forswear. Though Moscow hotels had already accustomed me to omelets of four eggs, the innkeeper's wife in Ust-Urda, out of deference for "the guest from America," made one from six eggs! When I failed to finish it, she, her husband, the other guests, in almost one voice, reminded me most earnestly that I was in Siberia and not in America, and in Siberia it was not the custom to leave unfinished an omelet of six eggs! Indeed it was not the custom to leave any food, omelet, soup, or meat, unfinished.

Heavy rains broke out at the time I was in this village. The roads were flooded, bridges were washed away, and for a week no bus came from either direction. About all the people in the inn did was to sit or lie around, tap glasses of tea from the ever-boiling samovar, and eat one meal after another—fish, eggs, meat, cheese, sausage, soups, in amounts that in any other place would have stamped them as professional gourmands. The Siberian appetite is not the least distinctive feature of everyday Siberian life!

Now agriculture is more than keeping pace with industry in Siberia. There are still vistas of virgin lands in the black soil belt that await the touch of a plow. Yet more and more of such lands are being broken up by tractor and gang plow, and more still will be broken up as the crowds of new settlers reach their destination. Rapidly the Soviets are converting Siberia into their second breadbasket, the first being the Ukraine. The summers may be short, particularly within and beyond the Arctic Circle, but the days are long, sunlight is abundant, and grains and other crops grow well—better, sometimes, than in European Russia. In the old days wheat, for example, was not known north of the fifty-sixth degree, now it is sown as far north as the sixty-seventh degree. Eagerly Siberian agricultural agents are disseminating the rich information that has come from Canada of the successful growth of wheat in Canadian northlands. Siberian laboratories scattered all the way from the rich belt of steppes to the tundras are tirelessly experimenting with wheat in the hope of developing still hardier and more productive strains.

The Novosibirsk region is agriculturally one of the richest in Siberia. In 1913 its sown area was three and a half million acres. By 1933 it had about trebled. Productivity had increased more than 50 per cent, so the latest reports indicate. The dairy industry is thriving. After the misfortunes that had befallen livestock in the early years of collectivization when peasants, out of sheer wrath, had wantonly slaughtered cattle, pigs, sheep, it was at first slow in coming to life again. But, once started, its successes have continued from year to year and in an increasing ratio. The nearly six thousand collective farms in the region average three dairies per farm. The average number of livestock per family is 8.5 heads—larger than the average in European Russia. Pigs and sheep have had an especially prolific increase. Here not only wheat but potatoes, hemp, flax, and cabbage grow in abundance, and more and more selected seeds are becoming the rule and the vogue, so that the yield may be further improved.

Here, also, is the beginning of a new horticulture. Except small fruits such as berries, which grow wild and in profusion in the thickest forest wildernesses of Siberia, fruit was and still is scarce. But the late Russian scientist, Michurin, had for years been experimenting with fruits that can endure the severity of the Siberian winters. His pupils have continued the work. Of apples alone there are now scores of varieties that will thrive in Siberia. All over the Novosibirsk region collective farms are setting out orchards—not a few trees, but hundreds and thousands of them.

The district of Narym, high above Novosibirsk and Tomsk, is an example of the agricultural rejuvenation that even remote parts of the Siberian continent have experienced. In the old days Narym was known as a penal center. It still is that. In my travels in villages in Europe I often heard of it in connection with kulaks who were sent there into exile. Relatives of the exiles spoke of Narym with dread and with sorrow, as of a place from which people never return. All faraway places of exile assume a more or less sinister connotation to people whose kin have been forcibly sent there. But the liquidated kulaks in Narym have been set to work. Tractors arrived there, gang plows, seeders, and other machinery. Work started on a large scale under the guidance of agricultural experts with experience in farming problems of the north. Forests have been cleared. New lands have been broken up by the sixty-horsepower caterpillar tractors that now dot the Soviet lands from one end to the other. Narym has become one of the most successful agricultural districts of the north.

In the old days the exiles and the natives never raised enough grain for themselves. They eked out a living principally from hunting, fishing, and gathering wild berries and wild nuts. In 1913 the sown area was less than

seven thousand acres. In 1939 it was 373,855 acres, nearly
all of it worked by tractors and heavy modern machinery.
The soil is rich, and all the usual grains are sown—oats,
barley, winter rye, spring and winter wheat. Dairying is
becoming an integral part of the collective farm, and for
the first time in its history Narym produces a surplus of
grains, meats, and dairy products.

The district is also rich in forests, in fish, and in furs.
Hunting and fishing are not only sports but professions,
and nearly every peasant practices both. As in other places
in Siberia, hunting has been collectivized, also domesti-
cated through the fur farms that have come into vogue.
In 1939 there were thirty-six such farms in Narym spe-
cializing in highly prized fur animals. Roads too have
been built, and villages are no longer cut off from one
another by endless stretches of mud and wildness.

There is the Cheliabinsk region, in the Urals, also renowned for its grains, especially its spring wheat. In 1913
its sown area was a little over five million acres; in 1939
it was almost eight million acres. The land is held by 2,921
collective farms and ninety-two state farms and nearly all
tillage is highly mechanized. Here land is so abundant
that the average area per family on a collective farm is over
seventy-four acres. The ownership of such an acreage in
the pre-collectivization days would have stamped a peasant as a kulak of parts. Here sugar beets have been introduced and yield exceptionally good crops. Livestock
too is attaining a record. The average in 1939 was 11.28
head for each family.

Situated in a land of fast-growing cities and industrial centers, this region needs above all else new settlers. From nearly every collective farm comes the call for new hands, new blood. No doubt hundreds of thousands of peasants and their families who have had to flee from European Russia will swell the much-needed population on the collective farm of this rich part of Russia's East.

The Altai region with its snow-covered mountains, its high, cloud-swept pastures, its interminable virgin forests of larch, spruce, cedar, birch, is one of the most picturesque parts of Siberia and one of the wealthiest. In size it equals the combined territories of former Estonia, Latvia, Lithuania, Belgium, Holland, and Sweden. In a preserve of two and a half million acres, game is abundant—bear, fox, squirrel, lynx, musk deer, Siberian stag, and the highly treasured sable. To the north and to the west of the mountains is a rich and measureless steppe, the very finest soil in Siberia.

The collective farms, 4,711 of them in 1939, have more land than they can adequately work with their sparse population. Here, as in every part of Siberia, the cry is for more people, more workers. The size of each farm averages 7,141 acres, or one hundred and sixteen acres per family, as against only twenty-two acres in the Ukraine. There are millions of acres that have never been touched by plow or known the tread of man. Here, incidentally, lives the young woman Sergeyeva, who has established a world record in wheat—growing nine hundred and six stalks to the square meter. Wheat land as superb as can be found anywhere on earth abounds in this region and there is excellent pasturage. Indeed it is one of the richest grasslands in Asia. The bee too is gaining increasing appreciation, and more and more collective farms are developing commercial apiaries. The climate is propitious, with cold winters, deep snows, hot summers, and abundant rains. The Altai is one of the coming migration centers in Asia.

The Krasnoyarsk region, in the very heart of Asiatic Russia, covers an enormous territory, almost one eighth of all the land in the Soviet Union. It was to this territory, to the village of Shushenskoye, that Lenin was exiled. It was also to this region, the village of Kureiko, that Stalin was banished. Not so rich in agriculture as the Altai region, it is one of the great forest lands of the world, stretching over an area of 417 million acres, the principal trees being larch, fir, spruce, and pine. Within the borders of this territory lie the mighty Siberian rivers: the Yenisei, 2,950 miles long, and the Lena, 3,114 miles long. In the north the land is perpetually frozen, and in the south in summer is hot desert. Here are some of the richest gold mines in the world, also the richest furs. Roads are scarce but are continually increasing, and air travel is widespread. Planes take off from Krasnoyarsk on the various journeys to the Arctic. The known mineral wealth is enormous; the unknown is still in process of exploration.

Here is one of the most rugged parts of Siberia and, like the other regions, is awaiting an influx of settlers— hardy men with pioneer spirit in their blood, with a love of nature's wildness, and of the travail as well as the fun of taming it to their own daily and enjoyable uses. Here too wheat is receiving special attention. The acreage sown in 1939 is five times as large as that of 1913. The tractor, the gang plow, the gigantic disk harrow, and the combine are conquering the earth. Especially notable is the effort to tame the Arctic tundra to productive use. Near Igarka, the thriving new city at the mouth of the Yenisei, is a state farm producing milk, meat, and vegetables for the local population. Formerly the diet of the natives in the north consisted chiefly of fish and game; vegetables were almost unknown. Now grain and potatoes are grown in increasing quantities though as yet not enough to supply all the needs of the local population. Leafy vegetables are likewise being acclimated, especially in the electrically lighted and heated hothouses, and cabbage heads attain a size that is rare in the milder climates.

The Krasnoyarsk region is noted also for its sheep ranges, its dairy farms, its pigs. Fruit is no longer unknown. Always rich in wild berries, these are now cultivated scientifically; two hundred varieties are grown on the collective farms. Apple orchards are being set out. Bees are becoming a part of the farm life of the country. More and more collective farms are starting apiaries, and the plan is to stock every one of them with bees and make honey one of the leading commercial crops. The flora is abundant, and although the honey-gathering season is short, it is of excellent quality.

The land of the Yakuts, Yakutia, or the Yakut Auton-

omous Socialist Republic, as it is variously known, is vast
in size. The winter lasts from seven to eight months and
the rivers freeze to a depth of six feet and over. The summer is hot and dry—the average temperature in July rising
above that in Moscow—and the days are long. In the zone
of perpetual ice the freeze reaches a depth of six hundred
and fifty-six feet. In summer the earth thaws deep enough
for planting. Drouth is scarcely a problem, for with the
ice below the plowed layer of land there is a continuous
source of moisture. Here too are deep and immense forests, chiefly of larch, highly prized for its strength, its
durability, its resistance to decay.

The Yakuts, who chiefly inhabit this land, form the
most numerous Siberian nationality. They are a rugged,
handsome people, and their students in Moscow and
Leningrad universities, with their finely wrought features,
their tar-black hair, and their snow-white teeth, always
attract attention.

The Yakuts have been hunters, foresters, fishermen, and
cattlemen. Of modern scientific farming and of the modern tractor and other agricultural implements they knew
nothing. Now both are part of their daily experience. In
1938 five hundred tractors tilled the land of Yakutia, and
the plowed acreage since the coming of the Soviets has
increased from about 100,000 to 250,000 acres. It is still
increasing! The crops are spring rye, wheat, barley, vegetables, and grasses for fodder and ensilage. New, well-
lighted barns have replaced the dismal little stalls of the

old days. Cattle are increasing in numbers and their quality is improving.

Nearly all the land in Yakutia, as elsewhere in Siberia, is collectivized, and the people here—Evenks and Russians in addition to the Yakuts—live more or less together, intermarry, and suffer from no national or racial conflicts.

I have dwelt at length on the agriculture of Siberia because it is one of the leading assets of the country. Though still new, the application of the modern machine and modern agricultural science is full of promise. Wheat, meat, dairy foods, wool, honey, berries, vegetables, sugar beets, hemp, and flax are produced in increasing amounts. In food, Siberia is more than self-sustaining in time of war and peace. Since the beginning of the war much of the high-powered agricultural machinery from evacuated territories has been sent there, and this year will witness the largest plowed acreage Siberia has ever known, especially for spring and winter wheat.

Collectivization has swept Siberia as it has European Russia, and because of that millions will be able to settle on the land with comparative ease. In the old days a settler needed a substantial amount of capital to cultivate a homestead. He had to build a house and provide himself with tools as well as horses, cattle, and other livestock. Now he need have little capital or none at all to join a collective farm. He does not need a horse of his own. Its possession is forbidden anyway, except in certain remote regions. The tractor station provides the draft power for the land and the most important implements. The collective or the government extends credit to a settler for a house and helps him to build it. He and the family can eat in a communal dining room and sleep in a communal dormitory from the very day of their arrival. The working members of the family start earning money immediately, except when they build their own house. Either the collective farm or some near-by state farm will sell a cow and a pig to a settler on credit. For children there is a school and a playground. In the clubhouse there are meetings, motion pictures, amateur concerts, and amateur dramatic performances. Of course the process of being uprooted is never pleasant. In wartime it is fraught with agony. But one can start life all over again in Siberia!

Collectivization has brought to Siberia not only the agricultural but the political and military features of the movement—rifle ranges, parachute towers, classes in topography, in military tactics, and in guerrilla warfare. The Siberian is especially adept in guerrilla fighting, for again and again throughout the centuries he has been called upon to wage it against native and foreign enemies. The popularity of hunting and the long season during which it lasts have kept up his skill in marksmanship. During the Japanese occupation of eastern Siberia, between 1918 and 1922, Siberian guerrillas wandered all over the occupied regions, massacred Japanese, and were in turn massacred by them. They made the Japanese realize that Siberians were a fighting people and would not readily submit to the imposition of foreign rule. The audacity of the Siberian guerrilla was in some measure responsible for the decision of the Japanese Government to evacuate the lands it had seized in 1918.

At present every collective farm is a school in guerrilla warfare, with even older folk making ready for the day when Siberians again face the Japanese in battle. This time the guerrilla fighting will bear an organized character even more so than against Germany in European Russia, for nowhere else has such warfare been so highly developed or so arduously prepared for. In the more eastern districts the settlers on collective farms are chiefly young people who have seen service in the Red army. They are in the reserves and train continuously. They literally sleep on their rifles, and the farms on which they live have been converted into fortresses. This is especially true of the border regions.

The new industry, the new agriculture, the new population that is coming there—mostly young, tough, militant, and trained for warfare—make Siberia perhaps the most powerful country on the mainland of Asia and the Japanese know it only too well.

CHAPTER XI

The Conquest of the Arctic

Russia is not only converting Siberia into a gigantic machine shop and a gigantic breadbasket, but is building an empire in the Arctic, a real empire, with farms, factories, fisheries, cities, scientific institutes, schools, theaters, and all else that man needs for everyday comfort and for holiday diversion. The work is still in its infancy, for it was begun scarcely more than a decade ago. But already, to a larger measure than was at one time thought possible, the geography and the resources of the Arctic have become a part of Russia's peacetime development and are destined to play an increasingly important role in the present or any future war that Russia may have to fight, especially in Asia.

The Arctic lands may never become the blooming centers of civilization that zealous pioneers are predicting, but never again will they be the scene of gloom and desolation that the world had for centuries imagined them to

THE SOVIET ARCTIC

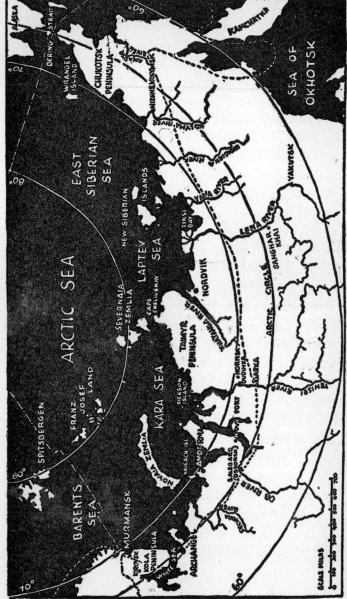

Broken line indicates mean isotherm of 50° F. of warmest month of year

171

be. If Japan joins Germany in a war on Russia and succeeds in driving the Russian armies westward, as far, for example, as the city of Irkutsk, the Arctic will become an important military base for Russian armies, particularly for Russian planes. A number of airdromes are already in existence there, scattered all over the far-stretching coast line of the Arctic Ocean. From these airdromes Russian bombers can take off, unmolested, for Tokyo or other large centers of Japanese culture and civilization.

The story of the Soviet conquest of the Arctic is as exciting as it is enlightening, and in some ways—if only as a means of ocean travel from Europe to Asia or of future air travel from Russia to America—is as important as the conquest of Siberia by the doughty Cossack rebel, Yermak, and his Cossack followers.

On several occasions in the middle twenties Vilhjalmur Stefansson, the noted explorer, gave me copies of his *The Friendly Arctic* to take to Moscow for presentation to Russian scientists. Because of Russia's immense coast line in the Arctic seas and of immense territories immediately behind the coast line, the Russians, Stefansson felt, would be especially interested in his book, the very title of which signalized a revolution in the thinking about the Arctic world.

The Russians were more than interested in Stefansson's experiences in the polar country and in his views on the prospects of building a civilization there. In newspapers and in magazines, in their own language as well as in English and in German, they had read accounts of his experiences and discoveries in the polar regions, which have always exercised a spell over Russian explorers and scientists. Some of them had traveled in the far North, in the forests, in the tundra, along the mouths of the mighty Siberian rivers, the Ob, the Yenisei, the Lena. They had associated with natives, who were hunters and fishermen, and had uncovered a condition of life that intrigued their scientific imaginations. Also they had come upon precious deposits of natural riches—coal, nickel, tin, gold, mineral salts, oil, fur, fish. These needed to be worked, made use of, transported to other parts of the country. But there was no easy way of doing it, or none at all.

Besides, the Soviets were embarking on an economic development which was based on unified planning of the energies and the resources of the country, of their Asiatic empire as well as of their European lands. Above all, they were thinking of war and of ways of fighting it to victory. The far North had not only material wealth which would be useful to the war machine, but held stupendous strategic possibilities on land, on sea, in the air. They wanted to explore and exploit these possibilities. First, they sought to establish through passage by way of the Arctic Ocean from Archangel and Murmansk to Kamchatka, Vladivostok, and other important outposts in the Far East. Once achieved, this victory over nature would be their exclusive monopoly and they could exploit it with great advantage in time of war, especially with Japan. Though the subject is never mentioned in official reports and in other writings on Soviet activities in the Arctic, there can be no doubt that military preparedness and expectation of a Japanese attack are in large measure responsible for the zest with which the Russians have been espousing the Arctic cause, which Stefansson, by the very title of his book *The Friendly Arctic,* was the first to champion.

On three different occasions in the past explorers had negotiated the difficult journey of the Northern route by way of the Arctic Ocean. They were Nordenskjöld, a Swede; Vilkitsky, a Russian; Amundsen, a Norwegian. But each was caught by the winter before he had completed the voyage, which was not at all what the Soviets hoped to achieve. The practical uses of the route would be negligible if ships had to lay up for the winter in a frozen sea. Therefore, after lengthy and elaborate preparations in the summer of 1932, the icebreaker *Sibiryakov* had set out from Archangel on this crucial voyage. In two months and four days it had cleared the Arctic Ocean and was in the Pacific! Russia was jubilant. Here was a triumph that held promise for the future.

The following year the *Chelushkin,* another icebreaker, followed the same route, but on reaching the Bering Sea it was frozen in. The ice crushed it. The one hundred and four members of the expedition managed to set up camp on the ice and to wait for rescuers. Here was a fresh challenge for Russian fliers, and they met it with extraordinary skill. After lengthy preparation and flying in gale and blizzard, they brought to safety every member of the party and all the dogs. This spectacular feat was another triumph over nature and further electrified the Russian people and enhanced their interest in the polar world.

Since then the Northern sea route has become an important passageway. Boats ply back and forth from Asia to Europe and Europe to Asia. Some go only to the mouths of the big rivers—the Ob, the Yenisei, the Lena, the Kolyma. In 1935 one hundred ships followed the Arctic route. They carried building materials, manufactured goods, scientific equipment, and parties of scientists to remote islands and to the Arctic coast line. Annually now the number of ships that follow the Arctic route has been increasing and not a single fatal accident has occurred to man or ship. In 1938 fifty-one scientific stations were at work in the Soviet polar region—on Franz Josef Land, Novaya Zemlya, Severnaya Zemlya, Wrangel Island, the shores of the Chukotsk Peninsula in the proximity of Alaska, and in many other widely scattered places. Since then at least fifteen more stations have been added.

Along the Soviet Arctic coast line there are now coaling stations, oil depots, food stores, everything else that ships or planes might need. There are new and growing settlements. The port of Igarka on the Yenisei, about sixty miles north of the Arctic Circle, is a city of 20,000, with sawmills, schools, a newspaper, a theater, and with an ever-increasing area of near-by hothouse gardens, farm lands to raise fresh vegetables, meats, and dairy foods for the population.

Farther north is Dudinka, also on the Yenisei, a fine harbor and the terminal point of the most Northern railway in the world. This town is some seventy miles east of and almost in a straight line with Norilsk, one of the richest mineral storehouses in Asia. It is especially rich in nickel, so much so that Russians hope to convert it into one of the great nickel centers of the world. Save for a few feet on the surface during the short summers, the ground here is perpetually frozen, but the railroad from Dudinka to Norilsk was begun five years ago, and more and more workers are going there. In addition to nickel there are rich coal deposits in Norilsk, also platinum and gold. Both Norilsk and Dudinka are farther north than the most northern part of Alaska, and Russians hope to convert both into modern townships with all necessary social institutions capable within a few years of accommodating a population of at least 50,000.

Still farther north in the Lapteva Sea, at the 74th degree latitude, is the cape of Nordvik. Originally this was only another polar weather station. But geologists have uncovered there oil, coal, and salt. Because of the intensive development of the fisheries industry in the Far East and all over central and northern Siberia, local salt is especially valuable. When fully exploited, Nordvik will supply nearly all the salt needs of the Soviet fishing industry in Asia and will stimulate the building of more canning factories there. In time Nordvik is scheduled to become another Arctic city, perhaps the most populous of all.

In the lower parts of the Ob, the Yenisei, and the Lena there are lumber mills, canning factories, and fur farms of increasing value, and more people are migrating there to develop these and other resources. Here is Sanghar-Khai, a town of which the world might never have known had it not been for the opening of the Northern sea route. It is about ten years old, has a population of over three thousand. Its chief occupation is coal mining. Though its coal is imbedded in a subsoil that is perpetually frozen, it is being dug with increasing success. Ships on the Lena pick it up and carry it north to the icebreakers and merchant boats that ply the Arctic waters. All around the town are dense forests, and it is more or less shut off from the outside world. Yet social services are on the increase. The town now has a school, a library, a telephone system, radios, a hospital, a post office, and a stage for amateur theatricals. It is also developing its own agriculture so as to be provided with fresh meats, vegetables, and dairy foods.

Following close on the heels of the establishment of the Northern route through the Arctic Ocean came the spectacular Soviet expedition to the North Pole, not merely to see it, as did Byrd and Amundsen, but to remain there, live there on an ice floe, and learn all that was possible about the condition of nature and life. It was on May 21, 1937, that a heavy four-engined Soviet plane flew over the North Pole and made a perfect landing on an ice floe. Soon afterward three more similar and several smaller planes landed at the same place, all loaded with supplies and scientific equipment. Four scientists pitched camp on the ice floe at the Pole—the first time such a feat had been attempted. By radio they kept in communication with the outside world, and for nine months they studied the ice, the wind, the depth of the ocean, the flow of the water, the organic life, which, prior to Stefansson's time, was not supposed to exist in the vicinity of the Pole. E. Fyodorov, one of the members of the expedition, in writing on this subject in corroboration of Stefansson's findings, says that at the end of July he saw Arctic birds. They soon discovered that these birds lived on small crabs, jellyfish, and seaweed. Then on "August 1, at 88° N. latitude, we saw some seals and soon afterward our camp was visited by a she-bear."

Driven by incessant gales, the ice floe drifted more and more southward, and in February 19, 1938, the expedition was picked up by Soviet icebreakers. The information they have gathered has been of inestimable value in the further exploration of the Arctic and especially in the promotion of Arctic aviation.

Long before the Russians established the Northern sea route for ships, they flew all over the Arctic. The auspicious beginning was made in 1925, when Gromov flew from Moscow to Peking over the Ural Mountains, the Siberian forests, and Lake Baikal. In 1927 another Russian flier, named Shestakov, flew from Moscow to Tokyo. Two years later, following a Northern route, the same Shestakov flew from Moscow to New York. These and other flights were for the purpose of testing, exploring, and establishing Northern air routes. The information the fliers gathered they imparted to the Soviet aviation industry, which proceeded to design and build planes especially suited to Arctic flying.

Then, on July 20, 1936, came the first nonstop flight from Moscow to the Far East across the Arctic. The fliers were three young men—Chkalov, Beliakov, Baidukov—who had been intimately associated in aviation. They flew in a specially designed monoplane, and the importance of this flight can be surmised from the fact that the public had not been prepared for it, did not even know of it until after the plane had already covered about one third of the journey. Deliberately the aviators took an extreme northern direction through Franz Josef archipelago, across Severnaya Zemlya, the mountains of Yakutia, Kamchatka, and the Sea of Okhotsk. The destination was the city of Nikolaevsk on the Amur, but the plane landed thirty-one miles to the northeast of the city on the island of Udd. It was in the air fifty-six hours and twenty-one minutes and covered a distance of 5,821 miles, breaking the then-existing flying record by some two hundred miles.

I happened to be in Russia at the time. The country, especially Moscow, went wild with enthusiasm. People called up each other on the telephone and showered each other with congratulations. Some of my Russian friends telephoned, asking whether America would be as happy as they were over this spectacular achievement. When I asked why they were inquiring about America, they joyfully replied, "Don't you understand what it means— bombers all the way from Moscow to Tokyo!" Russia was then engaged in a feud with Japan over the renewal of the fisheries treaty, and naturally people were thinking of the effect of this flight—pursuing a direction beyond the reach of Japanese fliers—on Japanese diplomats and Japanese generals. Suppers, dinners, dancing parties, and song fests were held in homes all over the happy city of Moscow. At a party in one of the Moscow embassies foreign journalists sought to obtain from the Japanese diplomats their opinion of the flight. But beyond broad grins and the endless repetition of the word "fine" they elicited no comment. Not even the completion of the Dnepnopetrovsk dam had given Russia such a sense of triumph and security as this sensational flight from Moscow to the island on the Amur River.

The success of this flight encouraged another Soviet flier, named Molokov, to fly all over the Arctic regions in a flying boat. Despite untold difficulties, he cruised around for a distance of 15,500 miles. Another Soviet flier, named Levanevsky, traveled to America, bought an American plane, took off from Los Angeles for Moscow, following a complicated route across the Pacific, Bering Straits, the northern coast line of Asia, across the Urals. On landing in the capital he had covered a distance of over 10,000 miles. These flights were intended to explore and establish fresh routes in the Arctic, especially a route from Russia to the United States.

Then came the most sensational of all Soviet flights. On June 18, 1937, Chkalov with his two associates took off from Moscow for America, flying across the North Pole, which is the shortest distance between the two countries. For years Vilhjalmur Stefansson had been advocating such flights. Now the Russians were actually embarked on it.

The plane was in the air sixty-three hours and twenty-five minutes, and for the distance of 3,665 miles it flew over ocean and ice field. It landed in Vancouver, near Washington. This flight thrilled Russia even more than the one the same fliers had made the year earlier. More than ever was the country enraptured with the achievements of the fliers and with the promise these held for defense against foreign aggressors.

A month later another Soviet plane, manned by Gromov, Yumashev, and Danilin, followed the same route, across the North Pole to America. Among other things Gromov was bent on breaking the nonstop flying record. This he achieved with ease. After staying up in the air fifty-eight minutes less than did Chkalov, he negotiated a distance of 6,302 miles, which was some five hundred miles more than the previously established long-distance flying record. Russia was more jubilant than ever,. though later this jubilation was dampened by the disappearance of a third party led by Levanevsky, who had also started from Moscow for America across the North Pole. Despite a diligent search by Russian fliers and by Sir Hubert Wilkins, not a trace of this party was ever found.

The military implications of the Soviet conquest of the Arctic even a layman can readily perceive. The possibility of flying bombers from America to Russia, across the North Pole, should conditions demand it, comes at once to mind. And these bombers can of course carry certain supplies. Passenger and freight routes can be established— like Stefansson, Russians say they inevitably will be—and make it possible for Russia to transport from America the more valuable metals, spare parts of machines, of planes, even certain kinds of ammunition. There can be no doubt that an established air route between America and Russia across the North Pole would have immense value for Russia and America in time of war.

Russian aviation in the Arctic means a new way of getting at the Far Eastern enemy. The Japanese, let it be noted, have had no experience in Arctic flying and for the simple reason that they have no Arctic territory. But the Russians have done more Arctic flying than any other people, and if driven from their Far Eastern bases they can take off from Arctic airdromes and fly to the Japanese islands with loads of bombs.

While the air routes in the Arctic make possible the bombing of Japanese cities from Arctic bases completely inaccessible to the enemy, the opening of the Northern sea route to the Arctic Ocean gives Russia another direct military advantage of no small significance. It makes possible the passage of submarines under their own power from Archangel and Murmansk to the Pacific or to Russian ports in the Far East. Most emphatically one of the purposes in opening the route was to make such a passage possible, though with their talent and passion for secrecy the Russians have never alluded to the subject in print or in any other manner.

In the Arctic Ocean there are no icebergs. The ice floes jam and crush against each other and against the coast line and the ice may attain a thickness of one hundred and twenty feet. But a submarine can easily dive down to a depth of three hundred or four hundred feet. Piloted by a plane, the submarine commander can keep continually informed by radio of the condition of the ocean, where the ice floes are, what their approximate size is, and where it would be safe to come to the surface again. With their love of the new and spectacular, it is more than likely that the Russians have already used the Northern route to send submarines under their own power to the Arctic waters.

Transportation in Siberia is a vexing problem, and the Northern route bears momentously on its solution. From Leningrad to Vladivostok, by sea through the Suez Canal, is 14,292 miles, and the canal might not be available to them, but by way of the Arctic Ocean, which none could prevent their using, the distance is cut to 9,940 miles. From Murmansk to Vladivostok the distance by sea is still shorter, only 6,835 miles, and the passage is all within the territory of the Soviet Union—an obvious advantage in time of war.

The railroads in Siberia are still comparatively few. There is the trans-Siberian which, beginning a little east of Chita, winds around Manchukuo all the way to Vladivostok at a distance of from fifty to two hundred miles from the Manchukuan border. It is therefore within convenient range of Japanese bombers, even now after it has been double-tracked. To overcome the disadvantage, the Soviets have for years been building a railroad which runs north of Lake Baikal to the sea abreast of Sakhalin Island.

The territory over which it passes is for the most part exceptionally rugged—torrents, mountains, forests, swamps, rock—often presenting engineering problems which have never been encountered in any railroad construction anywhere. The prospect of war with Japan has moved Moscow to concentrate all its energies on this road. Masses of political prisoners and others have been sent there to work, along with some of the best engineers in the country. Because of the secrecy which has shrouded the construction of this road, little information has reached the outside world as to the progress achieved. Perhaps it is already finished. Perhaps not. If it has not been, then with the fresh energies, capital, and labor poured into it since the outbreak of the war, it should be completed in the near future. When it is, Russia will have another trans-Siberian connecting the rich lands of central Siberia with the Far East over a Northern terrain that is not for the most part so easy of access to enemy bombers as the original trans-Siberian.

The Turksib railroad from Siberia to Central Asia, stretching for eight hundred and ninety-six miles, and the line from the trans-Siberian to the Karaganda coal fields, running for a distance of seven hundred and fifty-one miles, are the two new main lines that connect Siberia with the rest of Asiatic Russia. It is over the Turksib road that ammunition from Russia even now keeps flowing to the Chinese battle front, and the Japanese are powerless to stop it. There is, further, the railroad line—of which mention has already been made—from Ulan-Ude, the capital of Buryat Mongolia, to Kyakhta, on the border of Outer Mongolia, over which the Soviets will be able to rush troops and supplies in the event of an attack on Outer Mongolia. It is over this road that troops and supplies did travel in the summer of 1939 when Japan had attempted to storm her way into Outer Mongolia. There are numerous spurs and branches all along the main railroad lines which have never been mentioned in print and are a closely guarded secret.

Over the northern vistas of Siberia there is in addition to aviation much travel by water and by highway. The Ob, the Yenisei, the Lena, and the Kolyma flow virtually upward into Arctic waters. In summer ships ply back and forth on these rivers, carrying timber and minerals to the Arctic ports and returning with the manufactured goods that the ships there, traveling in the Arctic Ocean, bring from Europe or from the Far East. Under Soviet planning the rivers of the Siberian north—the Pyasina, the Yana, and the Indigirka—have been made navigable for the first time.

Nor are the river routes idle in winter. The age of steel, which the Five-Year Plans have carried to the farthest corners of the Soviet empire, has invaded all of the mighty Siberian rivers. Heavy caterpillar tractors roar along their thick ice, hauling large loads of freight. Caravans of long, heavy sleds loaded to the very top of their frames or higher can thus be transported with ease from north to south and from south to north. This gives Russia a new weapon or source of mobility, which in the old times was unthink-

able. Ships traveling in the Arctic Ocean can store away
for times of emergency all manner of supplies in Northern
ports and depots, and in summer as well as in winter
there are ways of carrying these to specially designated
places. Fighting planes, bombs, artillery guns, and other
armaments can be moved down or up the frozen river
beds as easily as fish, meats, stored grains, and other foods.
Soldiers also can easily be transported.

Under such circumstances, were a foreign army to fight
its way to central Siberia, a Soviet attack from the far
North, making use of stored supplies, might sweep down
and overwhelm the invader. This is only one more reason
why no matter how badly a war might go for Russia in
Europe or Asia she would remain unconquered, because
she would still have territory into which to withdraw and
supplies in the far North with which to strike back.

New highways have likewise been built in Siberia for
motor travel. As in the case of some railroads, not all of
them have been shown on the maps or have in any other
way been revealed to the outside world. There is a new
motor road now from Osh to Khorog through the Pamirs,
extending for a distance of four hundred and sixty-nine
miles. There is another in the heart of Yakutia, running
from Bolshoi River, a railway station near Chita, the center
of gold mining—to Aldan, a distance of six hundred and
twenty miles. In the old days the journey over this once-
primitive trek lasted twenty days, now it is negotiated in
eighteen hours. There is another important highway in
northern Siberia from Nogayevo on the Sea of Okhotsk

to the gold-fields of the upper level of the Kolyma River. Other roads have been laid in strategic territories, but, as already mentioned, not a word is known about them. All we know is that the millions of workers, political exiles and others, have for years been working on new railroads and highways, and that these have strategically been co-ordinated. On land, in the air, on sea, including the Arctic Ocean, Russia now has a system of transportation that gives her greater maneuverability in time of peace and war than she has ever known in Siberia.

Indirectly the conquest of the Arctic has placed at Russia's disposal a supreme military advantage over Japan. Weather is "born" in the North, and the numerous Soviet meteorological stations in the Arctic make possible decisive weather forecasts. The observations from these stations go by radio to the weather bureau. There they are studied, collated, interpreted, and diagramed. Since weather travels eastward—that is, from Siberia toward Japan—the Russians are in a better position to forecast the weather in Japan than the Japanese themselves are. For an air attack they can pick the day; perhaps the hour, they want—clear air with much wind—before the Japanese would know of it. An advantage like this can only add to the determination of the Japanese militarists to deprive Russia of Sakhalin, Kamchatka, and Vladivostok, and push her farther and farther from the Japanese islands, so Soviet bombers could not easily reach their cities with loads of fire and death.

There is another indirect military benefit from the conquest of the Arctic. It has made Russia the most Arctic-minded country in the world. During my last visit to Leningrad I happened to call on Ilyn, author of *The Russian Primer* and other books which have been translated into English and have found in this country and in England a large audience. As if to illustrate what is happening to the minds of children, Ilyn asked his six-year-old son what he would like to be when he grew up. Instantly the reply came back, "An Arctic flier." The romance of the Arctic has stirred the imagination of the Russian population, even the children. The Arctic Institute in Leningrad is a university for the study of every conceivable subject pertaining to Arctic life. Women attend it as readily as men and have made as good Arctic workers as men. The Russian language has become enriched by the word *poliarnik,* which means an Arctic worker, and which has no equivalent in any other language, for in no other country are there schools that prepare young people for careers in the Arctic. Consequently, there is never a lack of trained workers for expeditions to the Arctic. This in turn has made Russia more than ever look upon the North and on the cold that sweeps over it in winter with an indulgent, almost an inviting composure. More than ever do the Russians feel at home in the cold and more than ever do they learn how to live in it and with it in ease and comfort. The experiences of the numerous Soviet Arctic expeditions with all kinds of weather have been of priceless value to the army in training soldiers to fight well on the sternest winter days.

I have before me a book on hunting published by the Soviet Commissary for War, which maintains one of the largest publishing establishments in Russia as well as a chain of bookshops. This book is only secondarily a treatise on hunting as a sport or a profession. Pre-eminently it is a study of hunting as a means of military preparedness. It explains at length methods of camouflage, stalking and trailing animals, hiding from attack, and making every available use of the immense protection that a forest affords or that snow provides. But what is especially impressive is the discussion of clothes. Nothing is overlooked, no part of the body, no contingency in nature, no aspect of human physiology. The intent of the discussion is not only to teach hunters and everyone else how to dress fittingly for the coldest weather, but how to harden oneself to cold and to enjoy it for its own sake. If the Russian soldiers, in contrast to the German during the winter fighting of 1942, have found in the cold not an enemy but a friend, it is because of the studies and the experiments of the Red armies in Siberia with methods of taming the cold and making soldiers comfortable yet mobile in sub-zero weather. In this work, as already said, the army has been aided by the varied and cumulative experience of Soviet Arctic workers.

It is also in Siberia, incidentally, more than in European Russia, that soldiers have been taught to fight on skis, by day as well as by night, on the plains as well as in the forest. It is also there that they have had extensive practice in hauling on sleds, by hand if necessary, artillery guns, other weapons, and supplies.

The conquest of the Arctic, which is only in its beginning, is a further, even though an indirect, source of conflict between Russia and Japan.

CHAPTER XII

The Unfinished War

Nᴇᴀʀʟʏ a quarter of a century ago, without much loss of blood or too much substance, Japan came close to winning the most sensational victory in her history, infinitely more rewarding politically, economically, above all strategically, than was the peace she had obtained from Russia in Portsmouth, New Hampshire, in 1905, or the seizure of Korea in 1910, or any other military conquest she ever had made. She almost got possession of eastern Siberia!

Had she succeeded in that bold venture, the riches of that far-stretching territory—the fur, the timber, the oil, the fisheries, the farmland, the coal, and the iron would have been hers, to do with as she pleased. Russia would have been driven from the Pacific, far inland, and the task of her eventual expulsion from Asia would have been greatly facilitated. The Sea of Japan would have become a Japanese lake. The Japanese fleet, Japanese air bases, and Japanese armies would have been on the threshold of

Alaska, and America would have had to yield on issues in the Pacific or cross swords with a new Japan, bolstered by fresh strategic positions and by vast supplies of raw materials with which to pursue the war against America.

Thus, under the guise of helping the Allies and of protecting her national interests and her citizenry, Japan achieved a spectacular conquest in the Far East. So dizzying was this conquest in its implications, immediate and remote, that she fought strenuously to hold it even as Germany strove to hold the conquest she had wrung from Russia in the Brest-Litovsk Treaty.

Trotzky termed the Brest-Litovsk Treaty "a hangman's noose," because it left Russia and the Revolution almost at the mercy of the German army. But to Hitler, Brest-Litovsk was a "just treaty," because it was imposed by Germany for the benefit of Germans. It exceeded the expectations of the most fanatical Pan-German. It gave Germany hegemony in the Ukraine, the Baltic States, Poland, and the Crimea far greater than Japan had obtained in eastern Siberia. To Lenin the aims of Japan and Germany at that time were only too obvious. They sought, he said, "to divide and choke" Russia. No doubt this was their intention. No doubt this is their intention now. Their plans are bolder in conception than they were during World War I, though one need not be a prophet to foresee that if Germany, marching eastward, were to meet Japan marching westward, somewhere in the Urals or in central Siberia the two would inevitably clash in a ferocious war.

Yet despite their aggressiveness neither Germany nor Japan found it possible during and after World War I to retain Russian conquests. Germany lost hers in the defeat on the Western Front. Japan was deprived of hers by Russian guerrillas and American diplomacy. This is one reason why the two have ever since nourished a passionate grudge against Russia and the nations that were responsible for their one-time defeats.

The story of Japan's Siberian adventure reveals more boldly than the utterances of the generals her aims in Russia, her methods of achieving them, and throws an unexpectedly clear light on the unended war that the two nations have in one way or another been waging since the overthrow of the Czar.

On June 17, 1917, the Czar was already gone. The Bolsheviks had not yet come to power. They were still a clamorous and fighting opposition. There was a provisional government in Petrograd, now Leningrad, then the capital of Russia. On that day the representative of the Provisional Government in Vladivostok sent the following telegram to the capital:

"According to the information of the chief of our counterespionage here, Japanese gendarmes and agents of the secret police, posing as workers or professionals, have for some time uninterruptedly been arriving from Korea to Vladivostok. Several agents have come ostensibly to guard the director and the secretary of the Korean section of the Japanese Consulate against attempts on the lives of Koreans. Meanwhile, by request of the Japanese consul, a special guard of militiamen has been posted at the consulate. In such manner the Japanese are openly stirring up a dangerous situation. The same source reveals that the Japanese Government is taking swift measures to increase the enemy in northern Korea. Military supplies are being carried to strategic posts."

Three weeks later, on July 7, 1918, Krupensky, the Russian representative in Tokyo, informed Petrograd by telegraph that the Japanese were much concerned about the possibility of Russia allowing American businessmen to develop the oil and the mining resources of the Far East. The Japanese, Krupensky said, were willing and ready to undertake that development. They had approached the Czarist government on the subject but were informed that no foreign concessions would be offered in that particular part of the country. Krupensky ends his dispatch with the significant words: "The Minister (Viscount Motono) added that if such conversations with Americans have started, the Japanese Government would appreciate if they were allowed to lapse."

On November 24, 1917, when the Bolsheviks were already in power, the Japanese consul in Vladivostok, in protest against a threatened strike of longshoremen in the harbor, informed the local government that "if the strike occurs measures will have to be taken to protect the united interests of the consular corps in the city." Thus cautiously and vigilantly the Japanese were laying the groundwork for the impending invasion.

On January 12, 1918, the Japanese cruiser *Ivami* sailed

into the harbor of Vladivostok. The Japanese general consul assured the population of the city that the purpose of that cruiser was solely to protect the local Japanese citizens against possible harm.

On April 4, 1918, in the offices of a Japanese concern in Vladivostok, two Japanese were killed and one was wounded! This incident precipitated summary action though the Russians charged that "the murder of April 4 was the work of Japanese hands."

On August 12, 1918, 16,000 Japanese soldiers landed in Vladivostok and in Nikolaevsk on the Amur. Two months later, in October, the Japanese army on Russian soil was increased to 75,000. Still later it was further increased to 150,000!

The legal justification for the military operation was the decision of the Allies to intervene in Russia. President Wilson had fought long against the move. Finally he yielded, with the provision that Japan agree to send no more than 10,000 soldiers! Hardly had this agreement been reached, when Japan proceeded to violate it.

The ostensible purpose of intervention was to prevent Germany from gaining advantages in Russia at a time when Russia was turbulent with revolution. In particular, the Allies announced, they wanted to thwart the plot of the released German and Austrian war prisoners to seize Siberia and hold it for Germany. France and Japan especially kept proclaiming to the world that the danger of the plot was very great. Nor did the French and the Japanese swerve from their position even after Mr. Webster, a representative of the American Red Cross, and Captain Hicks from the British army, had made an investigation of the charge and found nowhere any evidence to substantiate it.

When it became obvious that such a justification no longer held any validity or appeal, the Japanese, again stanchly supported by the French, came forth with an array of fresh explanations and justifications. The Czechs were at that time in Siberia, and Japan posed as their "protector." She insisted also that Korea, Manchuria, and Japanese citizens needed "protection."

Meanwhile the United States sent an American army to Siberia as part of the Allied intervention. General Graves was in command of this army; his orders were to help maintain order without in any way interfering in the internal affairs of the country. Subsequently, in his account of the Siberian expedition, General Graves accused Japan of pursuing ends which in her official pledges she had abjured. Still later, General Graves's accusation found support in the testimony of a Japanese army man—Major General Nishikawa. In his *History of the Siberian Expedition* he writes: "As a matter of fact Korea and Manchuria and the Japanese residents in Russia never were in any danger." But at that time hostility against Russia was so violent that Japan's excuses and explanations carried conviction.

Unofficially the real purpose of the Japanese expedition to Siberia found expression in the Japanese press and in the utterances of Japanese military leaders. Thus the *Fuzan*

Nippon, a Japanese newspaper, admitted that Japan had to do something about raw materials. Unlike England, it said, Japan had no colonies. Raw materials were brought from the outside. Siberia abounded in natural wealth, and the Japanese people knew it only too well. Therefore it was no more than right that Japan should seek the exploitation of Siberia's natural wealth.

General Kairo Saito, in a book on Japan and America, reiterated this justification no less frankly, only he emphasized the military aspect of the Siberian enterprise. Japan, he said, must make herself independent of the outside world in time of war. In China and in Russia's Far East there was an abundance of raw materials to guarantee this independence. If Japan secured control of these "we shall have no fear of difficulties in supplies arising in wartime."

No sooner did the Japanese land an army on Russian soil than despite the pledge of non-interference in Russia's internal affairs and non-encroachment on Russian sovereignty they proceeded to do both. Russia was already in the shadow of civil war, and, taking advantage of internal dissension in Siberia and of Moscow's weakness to frustrate outside machinations, Japan launched an ambitious program of entrenchment. Her methods were as many-sided as her aims and no less ruthless. No sooner, for example, did Japanese soldiers descend on Vladivostok than Tokyo's diplomatic agents approached the Russian commander of the city with a proposal intended to bring the Maritime Provinces immediately under their control. They offered the Russian commander one hundred and fifty million rubles in return for an agreement allowing them to take over Russia's coast line, Russian fisheries up to Kamchatka, Russian iron in Vladivostok, and a perpetual lease on the Olginsk mines.

Simultaneously Japan flooded Russia's Far East with manufactured goods, as an immediate means of obtaining the raw materials she needed at advantageous prices. Then through intrigue with non-Bolshevik generals, especially Semyonov, Kalmykov, Horvat, and through terror against those Russians, whether Bolshevik or not, who failed to submit to the will of these generals, Japan continued to take over properties and to establish herself as mistress of the country. Railroads, cities, and villages were occupied by Japanese garrisons. In Blagoveshchensk the Japanese Military Staff took over ships, buildings, and shops. The Mitsui family came into possession of the gold mines in Suchansk district. Other Japanese firms gained control of the iron mines in the Olginsk region. In Chita still other Japanese business representatives came into possession of the power station. One after another the stores of this city passed into Japanese ownership. Fish and timber in the Far East kept moving in ever-increasing quantities to Japan.

Supported by the French, the Japanese embarked on far-reaching intrigues with White Russian generals for the complete control of the task of Allied intervention, so they could more easily entrench themselves in Siberia. Secretly the Japanese general, Nakashima, offered the Russian general, Horvat, all the assistance he might need in return for concessions that would have made eastern Siberia a virtual dependency of Japan. Northern Sakhalin was to go to Japan; mining concessions all the way to Lake Baikal were to revert to Japan; the fortifications in Vladivostok were to be dismantled and Vladivostok was to become a free port. Had it not been for determined American opposition the transaction might have been consummated and Japan would have acquired, at least temporarily, the legal basis for her military aggrandizement.

But American opposition neither cooled nor allayed Japanese ardor for the appropriation of the wealth and the lands of Siberia. Steamships in Vladivostok and on the Amur passed into Japanese hands. Soviet gold was shipped to Japan. In Sakhalin Japanese authorities nullified Russian law and dissolved Russian government institutions. They passed their own laws for the control of the private and public life of the people. By all conceivable legalistic and bureaucratic tricks they strove to squeeze Russians from ownership of valuable property or business enterprises. In an appeal of Russian non-Bolshevik intellectuals who at that time were living in the Far East, we read the following telling words:

"After creating a number of privileges for Japanese commercial and industrial activity, the Japanese High Command transferred to their countrymen fisheries, coal mines, forests, lands, oil fields, trading and various other stations, and squeezed Russians out as much as they possibly could. All sorts of obstacles were placed in the way of the Russian *entrepreneurs* even when they sought only to restore previously existing industrial enterprises."[1]

Japan therefore descended on Siberia not to aid the Allied cause, not to do any of the things she had officially promised, but to enforce Japanese rule and Japanese ownership, with the avowed aim of ruling through a Russian puppet, preferably a Romanov, if one could be found, or someone else who could be designated as a monarch precisely as in Manchukuo. Ruthlessly and with zest she was already practicing the racial capitalism that was some years later to become Nazi Germany's mighty weapon for the conquest of Europe, and that she had already exercised to the decided advantage of Japanese citizens in Korea, and that she was subsequently to impose on Manchuria. Here was the Fascist "New Order" in bold outline.

On April 2, 1920, the American army evacuated Siberia. During the time it had been there, it had on several occasions come almost to military blows with the Japanese. In the city of Verkhneudinsk, now Ulan-Ude, I heard endless stories of the conflicts between American and Japanese soldiers. Fist fights and brawls were frequent, and invariably the Russians took the part of the Americans. Though Russians are the least race-conscious people in the world, the depredation of the Japanese armies in Siberia has left deep-seated anti-Japanese sentiment, which transcends the bounds of political Soviet propriety. I was

[1]*When Japan Goes to War,* by O. Tanin and E. Iogan.

reminded of the anti-Japanese sentiments in the American Western states.

Nor was this sentiment expressed only in words. During the years of Japanese intervention guerrillas sprang up everywhere: in the forests, in the cities, in the mines, in the villages. Warfare was rampant. Villages often changed hands several times a day. Cut off from Moscow, the guerrillas could not obtain help from the capital. When they ran short of ammunition they raided Japanese ordnance depots or those of the White Russians. No mercy was shown by either party. Russian guerrillas pounced on Japanese soldiers and slaughtered them. Japanese massacred Russian guerrillas by the hundreds. Blood flowed freely, and the power of the guerrillas was rising. The longer the Japanese stayed, the more ruthless the imposition of their racial capitalism on the people, the greater the fury of the Russians, and the more savage the fighting. Though there was no official front, the Far East had become a blood-drenched battleground. The very geography of the country—the forests, the rivers, the vast spaces—aided the guerrillas and made it impossible for the Japanese to stamp them out. "The business-as-usual" formula, which the Japanese had hoped to achieve, fell to pieces. Trains were blown up. Caravans were set afire. The guerrillas were determined to make the stay of the Japanese as painful and as costly as possible so they would not find the venture profitable.

Meanwhile Washington was becoming more and more apprehensive and more and more articulate on Japanese aggression in Russia's Far East. In more than one way, Charles Evans Hughes, on becoming Secretary of State, reminded Japan of the violation of her pledge. Still Japan eschewed peace. She loathed the thought of pulling up stakes in a country which was virtually in her possession, which nobody at that time could wrest from her by force of arms.

Finally, with the help of Moscow, a buffer state named the Far Eastern Republic was set up in the Far East, and Japan agreed to negotiate a peace treaty with its representatives. The conference was held in Dairen, the port city in southern Manchuria. The demands Japan made on the Republic differed but little from the plans she had already carried out during the years of intervention. There was no recession from direct encroachment on Russian sovereignty or spoliation of Russian resources. The port of Vladivostok was to be put under foreign control, which, because of its geographic location, meant Japanese control. All fortifications in and around Vladivostok were to be destroyed and never again to be rebuilt. But in near-by Korea, Japan would retain her fortifications and all her other military defenses. The Russian navy in the Far East was to be scrapped, but the Japanese navy would freely sail in the Sea of Japan and in other near-by waters. The economic rights that Japan demanded are too numerous to be recounted here, but, if granted, would have made Japanese ownership and Japanese exploitation of Russian territory supreme.

The newly formed Far Eastern Republic repudiated Japan's demands. In this repudiation it was upheld not only by Moscow, but by Washington. Here was a rather strange situation. Officially Moscow and Washington were not on speaking terms, for Washington would not recognize the Soviet regime, and Secretary Charles Evans Hughes would not even receive the Soviet agent Boris Skvirsky, who had come to discuss the possibility of recognition. Yet, as had so often happened in the history of Russo-American relations, the two countries were face to face with a common enemy, and, despite their disagreements with each other, they proceeded to support each other in the fight against this enemy.

In desperate search of a valid reason for the demands on the Far Eastern Republic, the Japanese claimed that they had to be compensated for the loss of the lives of the Japanese consul and seven hundred Japanese soldiers who were killed by guerrillas in Nikolaevsk. The American secretary replied that the Nikolaevsk "massacre must be considered an incident." Still Japan balked. Eastern Siberia was too precious to abandon without a battle. Yet there was no way she could legitimately wage this battle without further rousing American opposition and intensifying Russian guerrilla warfare.

Hardest of all for Japan was the abandonment of Sakhalin. Here were oil, coal, and timber, which lay almost next door to the Japanese islands. There was much bargaining, much further intriguing. But it all came to nothing. Isolated diplomatically, fought everywhere by enraged guerrillas, Japan finally concluded peace with Moscow. The year was 1925, the place Peiping. On the signing of the peace treaty Japan withdrew her armies from Sakhalin and resumed diplomatic and trade relations with Russia. The only concession she obtained was a continuation of the right to fish in Russian waters and the exploitation of oil and coal in Sakhalin. Territorially, she gained not a span of additional Russian land.

The sting of the defeat remained, and Japanese generals never forgave America for her support of Russia in those crucial times.

In a pamphlet published for Japanese officers, entitled *The Real Tasks of the Imperial Army,* there are only bitterness and castigation for the men who were responsible for the capitulation. "During the World War," reads the indictment, "when the powers were unable to muster their forces in the Far East, were there no heroes in the Imperial army of Japan? It would have been easy to restore monarchism in Siberia and Mongolia." With monarchism in the adjacent territories, Siberia, Mongolia, and Manchukuo, the imperial principal, or "the Japanese imperial morality," would have been rid of all immediate opposition . . . and the destiny of Japan could have run along its own ancient political patterns. "Scared by the threats of America," the pamphlet goes on, "we shamefully abandoned Siberia and the might of the nation was lost for a long time." But Japan no more abandoned her imperialist designs on Siberia than Germany abandoned hers on European Russia. Both regarded themselves wrongfully despoiled of a richly won victory, and both bided their time.

The years between 1925 and 1931 were at most only an armistice between Russia and Japan, not, however, without incident and without acrimony. But while there were verbal tilts, as when the Russians closed the bank of Chosen in Vladivostok or when an attempt was made on the life of Russia's trade representative, there were no outright physical clashes. Beginning with 1931, when Japan seized control of Manchuria, the fight flared up again, and though officially relations remained unbroken, blood was spilled once more.

The Russians cherish no illusions about the Neutrality Pact they signed with Japan in April 1941, no more than they cherished illusions about the non-aggression pact they had signed with Nazi Germany in 1939. They knew then that Hitler wanted the pact for the sake of an immediate advantage, and they know now that Japan coaxed the neutrality agreement out of them likewise for the sake of an immediate advantage. The border clashes, which since the signing of the agreement have been muffled, may flare up again, as they did in the past, despite the armistice terms that the Japanese and the Soviet armies had signed after particularly violent border skirmishes.

The peace proposals which Japan has been offering China, if no other circumstance, carry their own meaning to the Russians. On January 22, 1938, Foreign Minister Hirota, in outlining such proposals, demanded, among other things, the abandonment of China's "pro-Commu-

nist," anti-Japanese, anti-Manchukuo policies and participation in the anti-Comintern campaign. Hirota knew only
too well that Chiang Kai-shek was no Communist, but
deliberately he used the word "pro-Communist" to dis-
credit the Chinese leader and to cloak Japan's intent of
drawing China into the fight against Russia. China spurned
Hirota's demands and went on fighting.

A year later Premier Konoye set forth fresh peace proposals for China, and this time not only was China to
recognize the "independence" of Manchukuo, but to
join in the "New Order of Asia" and the anti-Comintern
Pact, that is the Axis, and to help fight its battles. Konoye
proposed that Inner Mongolia serve as a special anti-
Comintern land, which meant that, like Korea and Manchukuo, Inner Mongolia was to serve as another military
springboard from which to launch the attack on Russia.

Once more China rejected the proffered peace and went
on fighting, and Russia has been continuing the shipment
of armaments to the Chinese front.

Japan's adventure in Siberia, like Germany's in European Russia during the lifetime of the Brest-Litovsk
Treaty, came to ignominious grief. In more than one sense
Japan's seizure of eastern Siberia marked the beginning of
a war with Russia, which has continued, on and off, to the
present day and which remains unended. It was an unde-
clared war like all the wars Japan has fought. Seldom was
there a regular or formal front, but the fighting, whenever
and wherever it took place, was marked by ferocity on
both sides. Russian guerrillas demonstrated even then,

in Asia as well as in Europe, against Germany as well as against Japan, their power to harass an enemy and to shatter local victories. Since Washington was as much, indeed more, the cause of Japan's defeat than were the Russian guerrillas, Japan's hostility to the United States gathered fresh flame.

CHAPTER XIII

Japan Must Strike

Neither Germany nor Japan has forgotten the spectacu-lar victories they won in Russia toward the end of World War I. Had they found it possible to hold their Russian gains, they might by this time have become masters of their respective continents—Germany of Europe, Japan of Asia. They certainly would have been in a political, geo-graphic, and military position effectively to challenge in-terference with this mastery. Then the fondest dreams of their haughtiest and most ambitious imperialists would have been in process of realization.

Nor have Germany and Japan forgiven the nations who compelled them to disgorge their Russian victories. In Germany, Hitler swept into power on the wave of what sounded an impassioned vow to avenge that "insult" to the German race and on a commitment to win back the lost victory. Hence his approval and justification of the Brest-Litovsk Treaty. Hence also his speech in Nuremberg

THE SOVIET FAR EAST: COMMUNICATIONS

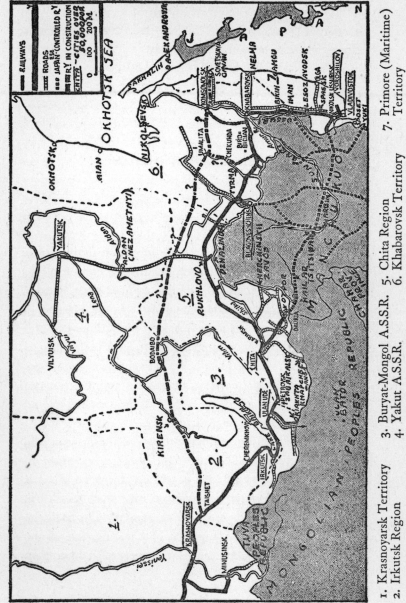

1. Krasnoyarsk Territory   3. Buryat-Mongol A.S.S.R.   5. Chita Region   7. Primore (Maritime)
2. Irkutsk Region   4. Yakut A.S.S.R.   6. Khabarovsk Territory   Territory

that if Germany had the Ukraine, the Urals, and Siberia, she would be swimming "in plenty."

In Japan the aim of fresh Russian conquests found expression in official and unofficial pronouncements of leading military men and statesmen and in the demands of certain influential business and political groups. Again I want to emphasize the speech of General Tojo, in November 1938, when as vice-Minister of War he bluntly asserted that Japan needed a high military budget so she could prepare for "simultaneous action on two fronts— against the U.S.S.R. and against China." In 1939–40 General Itagaki, Japanese Minister of War, in the debate in the Diet on the new military budget, likewise pointed to Russia as the reason for the rising military expenditures. Since, as I have already indicated, neither General Tojo nor General Itagaki favored at that time a non-aggression pact with Russia, which on paper at least would pledge both nations to a policy of peace, their allusion to war against Russia could have only one meaning—an attack on their Slav neighbor. Most manifestly to the Russian this allusion could have no other meaning.

Energetically Japan has been preparing for this war, especially in Korea and in Manchukuo, which borders on Russian lands. Between 1934 and 1939 the length of new railways in Manchukuo increased from 6,500 to 11,000 kilometers. One line leads from Harbin to Heiho, which is directly opposite the Soviet city of Blagoveshchensk, headquarters of one of the main Far Eastern Soviet armies. Another line leads to Halunashan, which ends on the border of Outer Mongolia. A third runs to Hulin, which is also close to the Soviet border. No doubt other short lines, branches, and spurs have been built but neither their number nor their location has become public knowledge.

Highways laid in all directions likewise lead to the Russian frontier or to the border of Outer Mongolia. Since the seizure of Manchukuo the Japanese have engaged many tens of thousands of Chinese laborers in the construction of railways as well as highways—Chinese laborers, I must emphasize, not Chinese executives or engineers. Next to Siberia, Manchukuo is the greatest boomland in Asia, and, like Siberia, its chief energies are dedicated to the production of "the sinews of war." Said General Gregori Stern of the Red army: "Immediately after seizing Manchuria, in 1931, the Japanese imperialists set about turning the territory of that country into a base for war on the Soviet Union." Airdromes are scattered all over the land. In 1934 there were one hundred and thirty airdromes and landing fields in Manchukuo. In 1939 there were two hundred and fifty of them. Since then the number must have further been increased. Fortifications of all kinds—barracks, stores, depots, arsenals, in all manner of camouflage, dot the land of the Manchus, which is now perhaps Japan's mightiest military stronghold.

Korea too has been harnessed to the Japanese war machine, in resources, in labor power, and in geographic advantage. Not so many years ago Rashin, for example, was a primitive fishing village, now it is a powerful port and naval base. Japan's armed forces on the mainland of Asia have risen rapidly. In 1934 there were in Korea and Manchukuo 95,000 soldiers and officers. From year to year the number has been mounting, until, according to Russian information, in 1938 there were 400,000 and a million more on Chinese territory. In Inner Mongolia, which borders on Soviet-controlled Outer Mongolia, the military preparations since its occupation by Japan have been intense and widespread.

On the other side of the border, in Russia, the preparations have been no less energetic. Siberia and Outer Mongolia push against Manchukuo on three sides—east, west, and north—and their borders as well as their hinterlands bristle with instruments of war, no less than do Manchukuo and Korea. The Russian cities of Khabarovsk, Komsomolsk, and Vladivostok are formidable fortresses, with all necessary subterranean passages and stores to repel an invasion or to fight a siege.

The port of Vladivostok is a highly fortified naval base. Since 1929 Russia has been maintaining an independent army in the Far East, divided into several independent sections, with all necessary equipment to fight an independent war in the event that European Russia, as happens to be the case now, is faced with a war of its own. Airdromes, landing fields, hangars—underground and overground; barracks, arsenals—hidden and camouflaged —are scattered all over the Far Eastern lands.

In central Siberia is another army and in the Urals still another. These armies, like the industries in the territories in which they are located, are the reserves to replenish forces and ammunition in Europe or in the Far East.

Russia and Japan are now precisely in the same position as were Russia and Germany after the signing of the non-aggression pact, August 23, 1939, or, better still, after the collapse of Poland, when over a vast stretch of territory no buffer land divided them any longer and they faced each other squarely as do Russia and Japan in the Far East. Officially, Russia and Germany were at peace, as are Russia and Japan now. Officially, they had almost ceased their campaign of vituperation against each other, as have Japan and Russia more or less so since the signing of the Neutrality Pact in April 1941. Officially, Germany and Russia protested good will toward each other, Hitler going so far as to assure the German people on September 1, 1939, that never would he permit another war between Russia and the Reich. Officially, Russia and Japan likewise protest good will toward each other, though not too often and never with a show of enthusiasm.

Unofficially, the non-aggression pact had changed nothing between Russia and Germany. Hitler had not even deleted from *Mein Kampf* his contemptuous denunciation of Russia and all Slavs and his threats to conquer the Ukraine for the benefit of the "master race." Unofficially, nothing has changed between Russia and Japan. Neither Premier Tojo nor any of the other spokesmen of the army who had been talking of war with Russia have renounced their former threats or have indicated in the military policies they have been pursuing a disavowal of former intentions.

Nor has Russia hesitated to show hostility toward Japan. On February 26, 1942, Maxim Litvinov, the Soviet Ambassador in Washington, at the banquet tendered in his honor in New York by the Overseas Correspondents' Club, proposed that the audience cable a message of congratulations to General MacArthur. This was not only a gesture of friendliness toward the United States, it was also a slap in Japan's face.

Unofficially, then, nothing has altered. The old issues between Japan and Russia have remained unresolved, precisely as they were between Germany and Russia. The armies face each other across a long-stretching border, precisely as did the German and Russian armies in Poland and on the Prussian-Lithuanian frontier. With hawklike keenness the Japanese and Russian armies watch each other across the highly fortified borders, which is what the Russian and German armies had been doing prior to June 22, 1941, the day Hitler attacked. In Europe, while Germany was at war with the Western nations, Russia had immobilized a powerful German army and air force. Now, while Japan is at war with the sea powers of the Pacific, Russia is immobilizing a powerful Japanese army, air force, also a substantial Japanese navy. Mistrust between Russia and Japan is as rampant as it was between Russia and Germany, and the Russian and Japanese armies that are facing each other in Asia's Far East are as much, perhaps even more, on the alert than were the Russian and the German armies in Europe.

Russia and Japan remain enemies just as Russia and

Germany remain enemies. Germany attacked, and Japan must attack before it is too late, else run the risk of finding herself effectively blocked in the fulfillment of her far-flung aims in Asia.

Japan knows only too well what is happening in Siberia. The new industry, the new agriculture, the new schools, the new universities, the new railroads, the new highways, the conquest of the Arctic, the gigantic steel plants already built from one end of Siberia to the other, others planned or in process of erection, the scores of new factories that are being moved from Europe—above all, the ever-swelling tide of migration, especially of young people, skilled workers, trained soldiers, doughty crusaders, are daily increasing Siberia's military and industrial powers. The new decree of February 19, 1942, banning the return of millions of refugees from the fighting zones in Europe to their homes, even when these are reconquered from the Germans, holds an ominous meaning for the Japanese militarists. Within a year or two the present population of Siberia of nearly twenty millions will be augmented by fresh millions, may mount to thirty and even more millions. This in turn implies a far more grandiose industrial and agricultural expansion in Siberia than original plans had envisaged, with infinitely more emphasis on military preparedness and national defense, particularly the building of air bases all over the country including the Arctic regions. From Tiksie Bay, from many another vantage point in the Arctic, bombers will be in a position, even more than they now are, to take off unmolested for Japan.

The new millions of settlers, with the vast program of industrialization and agriculture that they make possible, may give Russia an invincibility which no Japanese army in the future will dare to challenge—this regardless of the outcome of the war in Europe, for Siberia will remain on an active and even expanding war footing. Then Japanese ambition for the mastery of the mainland of Asia must come to nothing, and the vaunting dreams of Japanese generals and statesmen turn into a taunting legend. More than that—Russia's grievances against Japan, her mounting hostility to Japanese imperialism, her present avowed friendship with China, her refusal to recognize the seizure of Manchukuo, Inner Mongolia, or of any territory Japan has recently acquired by force of arms, all these must inevitably result in Russian support of Chinese efforts to regain lost territories including the ones newly conquered by the Japanese in the southern Pacific in which the population is mainly Chinese.

In his speech on February 23 Stalin deemed it necessary to stress at some length the Russian theory of racial and national equality. The German people were not the only ones whom Stalin had in mind and who will ponder on the meaning of his words. All the peoples in Asia whom Japan has conquered or may conquer will read their own meaning into them—a meaning which Japan with her behavior as the superior race of Asia, if not of the world, cannot help but find onerous and fraught with danger. Neither Germany nor Japan has grasped the indestructible vitality of national or racial sentiment, though no other nations boast of so much of either or seek so vigorously to inoculate their own people with both.

Soviet Russia's avowed proclamation of racial and national equality is a mighty diplomatic and military weapon in Asia, especially in time of crisis. Therefore, if India becomes involved in the war and Japan moves into India and occupies territories there, Russia's support of nationalism in India in every way she can, even as she is now supporting China's resurgent nationalism, will only add to Japan's worries and troubles, because it will add to the ferment and the rebelliousness of the conquered lands. An unfought and unconquered Russia in Siberia, from a Japanese standpoint, can only mean a powerful Russia in Asia, even if European Russia is in ruins. A powerful Russia in Asia must constitute a formidable military and political weapon against Japanese militarism and imperialism in Asia. Such a Russia by her very existence will spell encouragement of disaffection in conquered lands and will furnish armaments to vanquished peoples for effective resistance even as she is now doing in China. With a many-millioned and fast-growing population in Asia, with a swiftly rising industrial and agricultural output, such a Russia will do all in her power to thwart and paralyze, in one way or another, Japan's ascendancy on the mainland of Asia.

The continent of Asia is the richest treasure in the world. Its resources are beyond calculation, and they have not yet been adequately explored. More than one and a quarter billion people, which is more than half the human race, live there. The age of steel, except in Manchukuo and

Siberia and in certain parts of China, has only made its appearance. The commercial, industrial, and financial rewards it offers a conqueror are fabulous. Naturally Japan wants to seize it and hold it for herself, before anyone, including a victorious Germany, stops her.

In the last analysis the conflict in Europe is not dissimilar to the one in Asia. In Europe the flaming issue is whether the continent in the east and the west shall be dominated by a German master race or by the principle of national and racial self-determination. In Asia the flaming issue is whether the continent shall be dominated by a Japanese master race or native self-determination. On this issue there can be no agreement and no compromise between Russia and Germany or Japan. Already, with all the agencies of propaganda at her disposal, Russia is seeking to fan the sentiment of self-determination in Europe and in Asia.

Besides, the bases in Russia's Far East, which have hung like a nightmare over the heads of Japanese generals and people, remain in Russian hands. In time of war Russian or Allied bombers, with a system of weather forecasts superior to those at the disposal of Japan, can fly to the leading Japanese cities within a few hours. Nor can Japanese statesmen and military men disregard the possibility, even while the present war lasts, of an understanding between Russia and America for joint action against Japan. Such action would first and foremost result in the immediate bombing of Tokyo, Nagasaki, Yokohama, and other large and important centers of population. Japanese, like all other strategists, must count on all possible alternatives, even the very worst.

Perhaps it is his own uneasiness on this score that prompted General Tojo, the Japanese Premier, to announce on February 27, 1942, that Japan's northern defenses bordering on Siberia were so powerful that they afforded "absolute security." What Tojo means is that Japan is ready for the military showdown with Russia.

And time counts, for time is Japan's greatest enemy and Russia's greatest friend, especially now when industry in Siberia and migration are destined with the passing of every month to attain ever-rising peaks. Now, if ever, is Japan's chance, while Russia is locked in combat with Hitler's formidable Reichswehr and Luftwaffe.

True, Japan is also fighting on other fronts. But this fighting is more of a naval than it is of an army nature. Against Russia, Japan must fight chiefly on land, on the mainland of Asia, and the land armies in Manchukuo, seasoned from constant border clashes with the Red armies and from incessant drilling on the hills and on the plains of Manchukuo, are more than ready for the fray.

All the more important is it for Japan to cross swords with Russia while Russia is fighting for her life in Europe, because in nearly ten years of border fighting, including several large-scale battles, Japan has learned that alone she cannot hope to conquer her Slav neighbor. Otherwise she would have long ago embarked on an all-out war on Russia with a view to seizing at least the near-by Russian air bases and prevent possible air attacks on Japanese cities.

From none other than the Soviet general, Gregori Stern, who was in command of the fighting in Changkufeng in July–August 1938, we have an account of that battle. The Japanese, the Soviet general relates, had seized the heights of certain hills and were in a position to observe "literally every move of our forces." They had strongly fortified the heights and had woven thick barbed-wire fences around them. The Russians could attack only "along two narrow defiles, less than five hundred meters wide . . . every foot of these two defiles was under the fire of guns, mortars, rifles, and machine guns already placed and trained by the Japanese." The only way the Russians could hope for success was to storm these heights with all the vigor they could muster. This they did, using artillery, aircraft, tanks, and infantry. The attack started at five in the afternoon of August 6. By nightfall the hills which the Japanese had captured were back in Russian hands. Between August 7 and 11 the Japanese brought up new forces and "delivered about a score of attacks with the object of recapturing the hill." All their attacks were repulsed and then, according to General Stern, Mr. Shigiemitsu, the Japanese Ambassador in Moscow, requested Maxim Litvinov for an armistice.

Allowing for whatever partiality General Stern may show in his account, the fact remains that the Japanese lost that battle. They blamed it on floods, as Hitler blamed his disaster on the Russian winter. In both cases, of course, nature hampered the Russians too. Nor in the following year did the Japanese demonstrate any ability to overcome Soviet armies in their battle on the border of Outer Mongolia, and this time there were no floods.

From Hitler Japan will receive impassioned, indeed frantic encouragement. As already explained to Hitler, the conquest of Russia has become a matter of to be or not to be ideologically, militarily, politically. It is a question of life and death. Under no circumstances can he allow "swinish," "bestial" Russia to maintain the advantages she has wrested from him in the winter fighting. A "superior" race must expect only ignominious doom, if in the field of battle an "inferior" race attains the victory. Besides, his investment in Russia, in blood, in substance, above all, in personal and military prestige, is so stupendous that even if he willed it he could not withdraw without making the most supreme and desperate effort of his life to achieve victory. Therefore, Hitler must hurl against Russia every conceivable weapon and every division of men he can mobilize, directly and indirectly, in his own country and among his allies, particularly Japan. He will argue, flatter, goad Japan into an attack on Russia in the east, so as to divide Russia's fighting armies and make it easier for him to fight her in Europe. He will hold out promises and rewards without end, if necessary, and with his passion for melodrama, he will brandish over Japan's head the specter of doom—for both of them!

In November 1941 the German radio announced that "the military power of the Soviets has been broken. The

Soviets no longer can be regarded as a military factor."
Now, on the eve of the impending offensive, the German
radio is already announcing forthcoming victories. "Germany will defeat the Bolsheviks, and the Red armies in
Soviet Russia will cease to be a military power." The prediction is intended not only to uphold the morale of the
German people and Germany's allies, but also to carry a
message of optimism and encouragement to the Japanese.
Not that hardheaded Japanese generals can be persuaded
into decisive action by propaganda alone. But propaganda
repeated over and over does create often enough an illusion, if not a conviction. Through his emissaries in
Japan, Hitler will leave no argument and no trick unused
in the attempt to draw Japan into the war against Russia.
Most emphatically the emissaries, the hundreds that are
now in Japan, in one capacity or another, will stress with
all their powers of persuasion the timeliness of the attacks. "Now or never," "now as never before," "now as
never again," will and must remain the main effort and the
main weapon of their diplomacy.

Japan, of course, will be guided not by loyalty to Hitler
but by her own immediate plans and far-reaching aims.
Because of her victories in the southern Pacific she must
think with ever-increasing anxiety of the menace to her ultimate aims in Asia of an unfought, ever-growing, ever-
rising Russia in Siberia that never can accept Japan's
dictum of "Asia for Asiatics" and that will with every
diplomatic weapon in her hands fight its realization and
help others fight it.

Japan must strike at Russia in the Far East while the other end of the Axis fights Russia in Europe, or else forfeit all hope of ever becoming the dominant power on the mainland of Asia, perhaps even run the risk of being eventually pushed into a position of a second-rate power by the combined forces of Russia and an awakened and insurgent Asiatic nationalism.

CHAPTER XIV

Russia's Alternatives

IMMEDIATELY after Japan's attack on Pearl Harbor a cry arose in the United States for Russia to join at once in the war against Japan. The very editors, military experts, radio commentators, and others who six months earlier had doomed Russia's fighting forces to a speedy end, now wanted Russia to battle all alone the entire might of the German army and also Japan—some four or five thousand miles away.

It is not difficult to imagine the Russian reaction, not only of the Kremlin, to such an outcry. With their hyper-trophied suspiciousness, Russians, whether Bolsheviks or not, might easily have deemed this clamor as a plot to involve them in so much fighting that they would be destroyed or so weakened that their influence in the world after the war, and especially at the peace table, would be negligible! Anyone who has sought to cultivate an understanding of Russian psychology will, I am con-

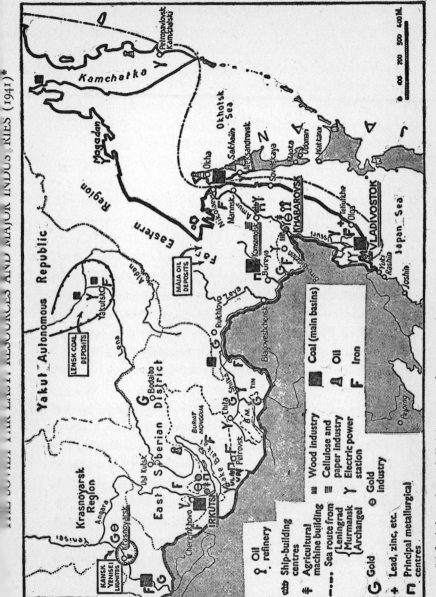

*Administrative subdivisions are shown as of 1936. For 1941 subdivisions, see map on page 209

vinced, concur in the correctness of this assertion. If we in this country readily leap to the charge of a Communist plot whenever a situation arises which only seems to stem from Russian influence, directly or indirectly, even if it doesn't, the Russians are no less prone to charge "imperialist plot," "capitalist plot" whenever they face a situation, particularly as vital as their participation in the war on Japan, which to them seems to stem from anti-Soviet influence directly and indirectly, even if it doesn't.

Some of the voices that clamored loudly for an immediate Russian attack on Japan may have had the ultimate defeat of Russia in mind. Others had not the least thought of it, were thinking only of a speedy defeat of Japan, which they honestly felt would be as much to Russia's benefit as to that of America and of the other Allies. But "fear," says a Russian proverb, "has big eyes," and suspicion, whether Russian or American, has even bigger eyes. Yet soon enough there were voices in America, in Washington, and elsewhere, which approved Russia's disinclination to open a new front in Asia.

Maxim Litvinov, the new Russian Ambassador, had arrived in this country the day before the attack on Pearl Harbor, and for nearly a week, while the clamor for immediate Russian participation continued, he remained silent. Then on December 13, in a statement, he said: "We are all in the same boat now, and will either perish together or together triumph over the greatest evil of our times, over the spirit of aggression of international infamy and barbarity." From these words it is evident where

Russia's sympathies and interests lie, at least for the present, while the war is on. But Litvinov offered no encouragement to those who clamored for immediate Russian participation in the war in the Pacific or to those who insisted that the least Russia could do in return for the more than one-billion-dollar lease-lend aid she was receiving from America was to allow America to use her air bases in the Far East, the only bases from which American bombers could make swift raids on Japan's large cities and industrial centers.

The question of air bases is not so simple as it sounds. Even if Russia were ready and willing to place them at the disposal of America, neither Litvinov nor anyone else with any degree of responsibility would make that fact known in an advance statement to the press as was demanded of him. Not being a military-minded nation, and accustomed to free expression of opinion on internal as well as external affairs, people in America often enough disregard the military implications of a subject in which they happen to be interested. It is quite certain that if America is ever to use Russian bases in the Far East, no advance announcement of it will be made, despite the ardor of some newspapermen to break the story at all costs to the public. No one in real authority, in this country or Russia, would be foolish enough to disclose such information to the Japanese and give them a chance to strike the first blow and to seize the initiative in the battle that was to ensue.

As yet America has not been using Russia's bases. Whatever other reasons may be motivating Russia's attitude, there can be no doubt that military and naval considerations are not the least paramount. To allow America the use of these bases means immediate war with Japan. The Japanese navy, air force, and land army will throw all their might against Sakhalin, Kamchatka, all of Russia's coast line, and against the far-stretching Manchukuo–Siberian border. Unless America is ready with a powerful navy to engage the Japanese navy, some of these bases may be seized—perhaps at once—and they will be used not by America but by Japan. Russia has a powerful fleet of submarines in the Far East, but nowhere near the powerful navy that Japan maintains there and for only one purpose —to fight Russia or anyone coming to help Russia. Is America ready to engage the Japanese fleet in the vicinity of Kamchatka or Sakhalin? Has America at present enough naval power for such a battle, which must be won else the much-wanted bases are lost, or are other commitments keeping the American fleet preoccupied in other parts of the world? Questions like these neither can nor need be answered publicly, least of all in these pages. They can only be acted upon and supply the answer indirectly through action. Yet it is an indispensable condition to any co-operation between America and Russia in the Far East, particularly if America uses Russian air bases.

Aside from America's naval readiness for such co-operation there are other considerations that guide Russia's actions. Like America, England, or any other nation, Russia is first and foremost interested in herself, her own welfare, and her own security. Nor are the Russians reticent on the subject. In a speech in 1934 Stalin declared: "Our orientation in the past and our orientation at the present time is toward the U.S.S.R. and toward the U.S.S.R. alone." First and foremost Russia's plans and Russia's attitudes are guided by self-interest, by what would best advance Russia's needs and Russia's safety, as the leaders understand them.

Viewed in this light it appears on first reflection that it is to Russia's advantage to fight Japan while she has powerful allies by her side, such as England and particularly America, rather than run the risk of someday having to fight Japan all alone. From long and bloody experience the Russians know only too well what Japan's intentions are toward them. They have not forgotten Japan's occupation of eastern Siberia nor the speed and the energy, the intrigue and the terror, by means of which she proceeded to occupy cities and villages and to squeeze Russians from promising business enterprises. No less well do they know that Japan's real plan in Asia is "Asia for the Japanese," and that once having failed to impose this formula on eastern Siberia Japan is not the nation to recede from such a purpose unless obliged to do so by force of arms or by other considerations almost as compelling. In countless books and documents, so that even school children would learn of it, the Russians have recorded and popularized Japan's effort to cling to Sakhalin, hoping that trickery of one kind or another would make it possible for her to hold it as a virtual possession. In the peace negotiations with the so-called Far Eastern Republic in Dairen she presented proposals which were intended to make her militarily supreme and unopposed in eastern Siberia. Too recent also are the memories of the battles of Changkufeng and Lake Nomonhan and the hundreds of other lesser border clashes between Japanese and Russian forces for the Russians not to know how irreconcilable are their conflicts with Japan and how inevitable is the final showdown by force. Most emphatically they have much to gain from an immediate settlement of the issue and from a condition of security for themselves in the Far East, especially if America is in a position to furnish necessary naval power to engage the Japanese fleet while the Red army battles the Japanese armies.

But Hitler at the moment haunts and horrifies them far more than do the Japanese. They know that in his quest for world power Hitler has forged two weapons which he thought had made him invincible—the Luftwaffe and the Reichswehr, his navy being no match for the British navy. His Luftwaffe failed to conquer the British or to terrorize them into making peace with him on his terms. At high cost of planes and pilots he learned that he was neither supreme nor invincible in the air. But he still had his land army. Country after country fell before its onslaught. With a swiftness that stunned and terrified the outside world, the Reichswehr swept on and on. Nothing could stop it. Like an uncontrollable force of nature it moved at will. It almost raced over France, flattening the "best" army in Europe into abject submission. Only when it turned against Russia did it meet a force that could fight it with a fury and a destructiveness which few Germans, including Hitler and some outsiders, believed possible. Amid blood and wreckage the Reichswehr rolled over Russia, reaching the very gateway of Moscow and Leningrad. It wrested from the Red army over 600,000 square miles of territory, an area about three times the size of Germany in the days before the annexation of Austria. But it paid a frightful price in life and substance. On August 23, 1941, only two months after Germany attacked Russia, Churchill said: "The aggressor is surprised, stopped, staggered ... . for the first time in his experience mass murder has become unprofitable." Then came the German retreat, neither disorderly nor without stout resistance.

The Russians know how powerful and murderous an enemy like Hitler's Reichswehr is—no other people know it so poignantly, for no other people have fought it or been fought by it so continuously and so savagely. Neither appeals nor ultimatums carry weight with besieged German soldiers. German garrisons in Kalinin, Klin, Sukhinichi, Andreapol, Toropets, said Stalin in his speech of February 23, 1942, were surrounded by Russian troops. The Russians offered them a chance to surrender and save their lives, but they refused. Naturally, many of them were slain. "War is war," remarks Stalin, and the kind of war the Germans are fighting in the rear more than rouses Stalin's wrath. The Red army, he says, is fighting "to liberate our women from the disgrace and outrages to which they are subjected by German Fascist fiends." Daily the Russian broadcasts carry stories to their people of the meanest and vilest atrocities perpetrated by German soldiers on civilians.

Therefore Hitler to the Russians is and must remain public enemy number one, as Litvinov has expressed himself. No one else spells so much evil, and it is he and all that he represents that they are determined to destroy first. If they have to choose between abandoning Vladivostok to the Japanese or Moscow to Hitler, they will choose the first alternative. With Hitler out of the way, the task of smashing the Axis in their view becomes neither formidable nor even difficult. He *is* the Axis; without him it falls apart like the staves of an unhooped barrel. So the Russians hold.

They also know that he is still mighty and is energetically gathering his might for the fiercest effort he has yet made on the battlefield. "Hitler knows," said Litvinov, "that either he will win this campaign and win all or he will lose it and lose all."

He has one stupendous advantage over Russia—greater industrial power. He has not had to blow up cities, factories, and dams, as they have done. Not a single blacksmith shop in the territories which he rules did he have to explode into smoke and cinders; not a stalk of wheat did he have to set afire. Therefore for the Russians with their inferior industrial output to fight Hitler and the Japanese at the same time and thus divide their fighting energies between two fronts four or five thousand miles apart, is to invite catastrophe, perhaps the greatest Russia has known.

They have grumbled openly and ominously at the need of fighting Hitler all alone on land. In his speech on February 23 Stalin alluded to the fact that Hitler had Italy, Finland, Rumania as Allies, actually participating in the campaign against Russia, whereas "the Red army, so far, has no such support." Litvinov amplified bluntly and dramatically the full meaning of Stalin's words. He said, "It may be of little use to have large, well-equipped armies, say somewhere in the west, if they are not in action while decisive battles are raging in the east. When such battles are over it may be too late for the western armies to serve their purpose."

So instead of Russia dividing her armies between two faraway battlefields, the Russians are urging the Allies to fight Hitler on every possible front so as to ease their task of dealing with his legions, most of which they will have to battle.

And yet it is not impossible, despite their protestations, that they will participate in an offensive in the Far East even while they are fighting Hitler. Nothing the English-speaking countries, and especially America, seek so much as an effective way of taking the war to the Japanese islands, such as Russian participation would at once make possible. The initial successes of the Japanese in the southern Pacific have more than rankled Washington and London. They want to avenge the defeat they have suffered and to visit on Japan the horror she has dealt to others with such a lavish hand. It is therefore within the realm of probability that an agreement will be reached with Moscow for them to open a front in the west so as to ease Russia's task of fighting Hitler, in return for Russian participation in the east so as to afford them the chance to carry the war with all the weapons they can gather directly to the cities and the industrial centers of Japan.

Japan must be keenly aware of such a possibility, and that is another reason why she may perpetrate a Pearl Harbor on Vladivostok and other Russian possessions in the Far East.

Of one thing we may be certain—whoever strikes the first blow will do so without a hint or warning.

CHAPTER XV

The Battle unto Death

WHAT MAY BE the outcome of a war between Russia and Japan?

Definite prediction at this time of immediate results is of course impossible. Too many are the unknown facts; too obscure or as yet nonexistent are the imponderables inherent in any modern war; too intimately is a war between Russia and Japan destined to be linked with the other wars that the Axis and the United Nations may be fighting. After all, this is a global and not a local war. By their pact of September 27, 1940, Germany, Japan, and Italy have become allies. Suppose the Axis breaks up? Suppose the United Nations fail to hold together? Suppose revolution flares up in Italy, in France, in Rumania, in any other country? Nothing is impossible. One can only venture an estimate of certain immediate forces in a Russo-Japanese war and of possible long-range eventualities.

We must start with the fact that for nearly ten years,

by means of hundreds of bloody border skirmishes, Japan has sought to feel out the weak links in the Russian far-flung line of defense. She had hoped to uncover many such links, break through them, expel Russia from the Maritime Provinces, or push her farther west. Yet no-where did the longed-for weak links show themselves. On the three known occasions when the skirmishes be-came battles, only once, in 1937, on the Amur River, did the Russians withdraw their forces from disputed terri-tory and agree to the *status quo ante*—which was no more of a victory for Japan than it was a defeat for Russia. In the battle of Changkufeng, in July–August 1938, the Japanese drove the Russians from the heights of dis-puted hills, but the Russians recaptured these heights and the Japanese were unable to dislodge them again and agreed to an armistice.

In the battle at Lake Nomonhan, on the border of Outer Mongolia, the bloodiest the two armies have fought, Japanese spokesmen admitted that Russian me-chanical equipment was superior to their own. Japan, therefore, has learned that the Russian armies in the Far East possessed strength which Japanese generals did not think they could easily shatter.

But now Russia is involved in a life-and-death struggle with Germany and Japan is involved in a war in the Pacific. Yet the forces Russia is facing in Europe are infinitely more formidable than those Japan is facing in Asia. The Allied nations in the southern Pacific have no-where near the military power that Germany can muster for a fresh offensive against the Red armies. For this reason alone one must assume that Russia has not seriously if at all weakened her military forces in the Far East, which in turn must oblige Japan to keep up her usual strength in that part of the world. The reports of Siberian troops fighting in European Russia do not necessarily mean that such troops came from the Far East, no more than reports of Japanese troops from Manchukuo fighting in China and in the southern Pacific mean that Japan has seriously if at all depleted the armed forces assigned to the Manchukuo–Siberian border.

Siberia has been a vast training base and testing ground for Russian troops, and Manchukuo has served a similar purpose for the Japanese troops. The reserves in either place are at the disposal of an army already at war or preparing for war, to replenish devastated or weakened forces or to augment those already fighting.

It is unthinkable that either Russia or Japan would jeopardize her military position in the Far East by withdrawing enough troops to give the other an immediate advantage. They might have done so with some degree of safety had they trusted the Neutrality Pact which they signed in April 1941. But Russia and Japan are not likely to waste such trust on each other, no more than Germany and Russia wasted any trust on each other after signing their non-aggression pact. It was during the life of this pact that Russia and Germany fortified themselves for the war which Hitler launched on June 22, 1941.

Geographically Japan enjoys an obvious and decided

advantage over Russia in the Far East. She is closer to her bases of supplies. Transportation in Korea and Man-chukuo, as well as by water in the Sea of Japan, is more highly and more advantageously developed than in Siberia. Japan can shift troops and equipment more rapidly than can Russia, because she has more railroads and more highways to the Siberian border than Russia has to the Manchukuan border. To offset these advantages of the Japanese, the Russians have for years been storing vast supplies of food, fuel, and armaments in convenient and reachable depots.

In a war in the air Japan's geography places her at a serious disadvantage. Japan's large cities and industrial centers are within easy bombing distance from Russian bases, while Russia's chief industrial centers in Siberia are scattered and far away from Japanese bases. Russia has seven important cities in the Far East: Petropavlovsk-Kamchatskii, Vladivostok, Khabarovsk, Komsomolsk, Blagoveshchensk, Nikolayevsk, and Chita. These are within comparatively short range of Japanese bombers flying from bases on the Japanese islands, Manchukuo, or Korea. The largest of these cities, according to the census of 1939, is Vladivostok, with a population of 206,-432. Since 1939 there has been a rising tide of migration to the Far East, especially to the city of Komsomolsk, the leading industrial center in the region. Yet at most the aggregate population of these cities is only somewhat larger than is the population of Mukden, the most popu-us city in Manchukuo, and hardly as large as the population in the Japanese city of Kobe, which, according to the latest figures, is 1,006,100.

Most of these Russian cities, especially those on the rim of the Sea of Japan like Vladivostok, or on the border of Manchukuo like Blagoveshchensk, are highly fortified. The other Russian cities in Siberia, beginning with Irkutsk and all the way to Sverdlovsk in the Urals, are so widely scattered and so far from Japanese bases that, with the possible exception of Irkutsk and Ulan-Ude and the steel city of Petrovsk, they are completely beyond the reach of Japanese bombers, unless Japan seizes all of eastern Siberia. Even then the cities of central Siberia and the Urals are superbly protected by distance alone from air attacks.

But Japan is in no such a happy position. All her cities on the Japanese islands and in Manchukuo and Korea are within easy flying distance from Russian bases. Nor is there anywhere in all of Russian Asia a single city with as large a population as are the leading cities of Japan. Tokyo has a population of 7,094,600; Yokohama, 866,000; Nagoya, 1,249,100; Kobe, 1,006,100; Kyoto, 1,177,200; Osaka, 3,394,200. Not one city in Siberia or the Urals has attained a population of a million, and only two, Novosibirsk and Sverdlovsk, have by this time grown to half a million each. Unless the Russians are swiftly driven inland, they can visit frightful punishment on Japanese cities and industries—infinitely more frightful than the Japanese can visit on their cities and industrial centers. Besides, if Russia is driven from her present bases in the Far East, she can still carry on bombardments of Japanese cities from the utterly inaccessible Arctic bases.

If the worst comes, the very worst, and Japan pushes Russia west of Lake Baikal, and Germany, fighting in Europe, throws Russia across the Volga and pushes her toward the Urals, Russia still is not defeated. It is this writer's judgment that complete or lasting victory over present-day Russia is unattainable either by Japan or Germany or both of them, regardless of how heavy are Russian losses in territory, in substance, in blood. The Russia of 1928 might have been completely vanquished, but not the Russia of 1942! This may seem like a foolhardy pronouncement, yet the facts are compelling enough. None other than Hitler, in speaking of the German-Russian fighting in World War I, says in *Mein Kampf* (p. 256):

"For three years now these Germans had stormed Russia, at the beginning without even the slightest seeming success. One almost laughed at this senseless enterprise; because, by the overwhelming number of his men, the Russian giant was finally sure to remain the victor, Germany, however, would collapse after having bled herself out. . . . Was not the day to arrive when, after the last German victory, still not the last Russian armies would march up for the very last battle? And what then? In all human probability, a Russian victory could well be postponed, but it was bound to come."

In this declaration Hitler recognizes the invincibility of Russian numbers even as in the same *Mein Kampf* he recognizes the invincibility of Russian geography and

Russian space. If, in spite of these words, he launched his attack on Russia, it is because, like the German and nearly all the other foreign diplomats in Russia, he had grossly underestimated the achievements of the Revolution and particularly of the three Five-Year Plans. ". . . Russia, which even today can still not call its own," he wrote in *Mein Kampf,* "a single factory in which can be manufactured a motor vehicle that really runs." Though prior to the outbreak of the present war Russia had some of the largest motor factories in Europe, Hitler had evidently believed that his words in *Mein Kampf* were still substantially correct. The continuous and vehement denunciations of factory inefficiency in the Russian press had only substantiated the opinions and the judgments of German and other foreign representatives in Moscow, that the modern machine age was beyond the efficient grasp of the "volatile," "romantic," "argumentative," "undisciplined," "slovenly" Russian.

Obviously Hitler was convinced that the Russian Plans in terms of achievement were a failure, at least to the extent that under no circumstances could the Russians hold up against the magnificent industrial system that was at his command and the superb military leadership and military organization which the Reichswehr had attained. Overwhelming was the opinion, not only in Germany but in nearly all foreign countries, in support of this judgment. The power of the Soviet idea, of the Soviet machine, of the Soviet organization, appeared to Hitler as something unworthy of serious esteem. Therein lay his chief error.

If driven from eastern Siberia by Japan and from Europe by Germany, the Russians will still have the Urals, central Siberia, Central Asia, and their Arctic empire from which to continue waging war. They will have armaments and food in these lands, though in the rear, in the occupied regions, there may be famine. I cannot conceive of Hitler, *under the best of circumstances,* being in a position to perform the miracle of forcing his way *into* the Urals, no more than I can imagine Japan performing the miracle of forcing her way *into central Siberia.* Both Axis powers will have overextended lines to protect, and, as far as Russia is concerned, guerrilla warfare will be rampant and bloody and will give the occupied forces neither peace nor rest. Unless Russia is driven from the Urals or conquered there as well as in central Siberia, neither Germany nor Japan can hope to achieve final or lasting victory.

The Russia of today is not the Russia of the days of Brest Litovsk in 1918, when she capitulated to the strangling treaty which Germany imposed on her. *That* Russia had no choice. The country everywhere was disorganized. The Soviets had internal enemies at every hand, some openly conspiring with the invader. The Bolsheviks had swept into power, but the fight to keep the power was still ahead. Industry was in confusion, in some places completely paralyzed. Agriculture was in no better state. The Soviets had no complete control of either, of agriculture almost none at all, as the requisition parties they sent out to the villages so amply testify. Nor did they have a well-trained army. The Russian army, even more than Russian industry, was in process of disintegration, had all but collapsed. The very method the Bolsheviks used to hoist themselves into power—the class war—had fostered and hastened this disintegration.

The leaders were afire with ideas, but none of them had any experience in the practical ways of the world— in industry, in agriculture, in transportation, in finance, in government, in all else by which a people lives. They were amateurs in everything, above all in military affairs. They could not begin to stand up against the formidable military machine that the Kaiser's Reichswehr had flung at them, supported as it was by a smoothly functioning industrial system, by a perfected military organization, by the German people, including the Social Democrats, who were too good Germans to be good Socialists and had no scruple in upholding, though only indirectly, the murderous Brest-Litovsk Treaty. Besides, the Soviets *did* have the formidable internal task of overcoming their "class enemies," that is, of fighting it out with the groups that violently opposed them and continually conspired to overthrow them.

It is all different now. A quarter of a century of revolution and three Five-Year Plans have changed the very face of the country. Inordinate has been the cost of the change, but momentous has been its significance. Russia is paying a gruesome price in the present war, far more than any other of the United Nations, conquered or unconquered. If Germany ever throws the Russian armies across the Volga or clears them out of Europe, and if Japan, driving from the east, pushes them beyond Lake Baikal, Russia will have been horribly devastated, profusely bled, but she will, I must repeat, still have a mighty industry and a mighty agriculture in the Urals, in central Siberia, in Central Asia. Including the Arctic, she will still sprawl over a territory larger than all of Europe. She will also have an army of millions. With her enormous man power she will be continually training new millions; and since the war with Germany Siberia has been her chief training ground. Besides, during the first five months of war with Germany, when the Red armies were retreating, the main forces managed to escape encirclement. Try as hard as they might the Germans seldom succeeded in bringing their crushing steel pincers together around these forces. Now that the Russians have had enormous experience in fighting the Reichswehr it is only logical to suppose that they will even more often manage to elude the German pincers should Germany succeed in spreading them out once more. Russian armies may retreat again. Some of them may be destroyed. But not all. If Hitler couldn't achieve the feat of destroying the Russian armies in his first offensive, it is hardly possible that he will be able to do so in any other offensive. Besides, there always will be the millions of reserves in Siberia. Nor has Hitler enough soldiers, and he never will have, to guard the far-flung borderline of occupied parts of Russia. Young people, men and women, soldiers and others, will find ways of slipping out and joining the Russian forces, wherever they may be. Presumably also Russia will have allies that will keep both Germany and Japan fighting on other fronts, which will ease her military burdens.

The leadership of present-day Russia is not made up of amateurs, neither in industry, in agriculture, in government, in finance, least of all in the army. It is made up of men trained and hardened by harsh experience and impassioned resoluteness. Nor has Russia now to worry about "class enemies." The central government has complete control of agriculture, of industry, of everything. The predictions of professional Sovietophobes that the Russian people would find in this war the much-longed-for opportunity for revenge on the Soviets or on Stalin have fallen by the wayside. The civilian population everywhere has been armed for guerrilla warfare in which it has for years been educated. It has used these arms for the purpose for which they were intended—fighting German soldiers on Russian soil—by day and even more by night.

Nowhere among the native inhabitants has Hitler been able to rouse support in the conquered parts of Russia. The German radios at Smolensk, Kiev, Warsaw, Bratislava, Breslau, and Königsberg keep shouting to the Russian population that Germany means only to cleanse Russia of "Jews" and of "monsters" like Stalin and Voroshilov, but there is no response. The very behavior of the German soldiers stirs fiery antagonism and hate. The Germans drive Russians from their homes. They seize available food whenever they can lay hands on it. They slaughter livestock. They desecrate historic shrines such as Tolstoy's home in Yasnaya Poliana, Tchaikovsky's home in Klin, Chekhov's in Taganrog. They seize warm bedding and warm clothes. They hang, torture, and shoot civilians. I don't believe there is a single village which has been under German occupation but has at least one martyred person, usually a youth, often enough a girl, whom German soldiers have strung up on gallows or shot, and who has become the symbol of Russian heroism and of German villainy. It is well enough for Stalin and for the Russian radio to proclaim loudly to the German people and to the world that the Russians are not fighting Germans as such, but only the Hitlerite clique. This may be much-needed and excellent propaganda. In a basic sense it may also be true. But to the peasants who have been robbed of their food, their livestock, their warm clothes, who have been driven from their homes, whose son or daughter, father or mother, whether a guerrilla or not, has been beaten to death or hanged or shot, the distinction has little meaning. Whatever the Russian might feel about the Germans in Germany, the Germans on Russian soil are his mortal enemies, and against them he will battle with every weapon at his command and with all the hate in his soul.

The Russian radio recites daily to the people story after story of German atrocities. The Russian motion pictures show daily to millions examples of such atrocities taken in reconquered villages and cities. Some of these examples are too horrible to describe. Under the circumstances, there can be neither forgiveness nor will-

ingness to forgive Germans their misdeeds and their
depredations on the part of the common folk of Russia.
Quite obviously, if Russian leaders were planning a
separate agreement with Hitler at the expense of their
allies or their own people, as news stories and certain
American writers and military "experts" keep continually
implying, they would not seek to keep afire the hate of
the invader and the fighting spirit of the masses. Neither
the radio nor the motion-picture houses would be daily
dramatizing German barbarities.

The Quisling or Vichyite government, which we were
told would come into being once Hitler had reached
Moscow, has made no appearance anywhere in the occupied territory, though at the height of German victories
it embraced an area three times the size of Germany prior
to the annexation of Austria. It held a population larger
than that of France. This population was made up chiefly
of peasants who, we were assured, would be among the
first to desert the Soviets. Yet despite the chicanery, the
bluff, the terror the Germans have unleashed in the conquered Russian territories they have been unable to find a
Pétain, a Laval, a Darlan among the Soviet Russians, not
even a Dr. Hacha!

Nothing would have been easier than for these Russians
to revolt against Moscow and proclaim their independence,
even as Fascist Slovaks have done in former Czechoslovakia and as Fascist Croats have done in former Yugo-
slavia. Nothing would have been welcomed by the
Germans more readily and more cheerfully. Indeed, there

is nothing they have more energetically striven to achieve, so as to be in a position to proclaim to the world and to their own people that Russians gladly rise up against the "Bolshevik monster" and welcome the German "liberator." Nothing would have placed in Hitler's hands so extraordinary a moral weapon with which to justify his "crusade" against "godless" and "barbarous" Moscow. Yet the revolt has signally failed to materialize.

At first the Nazis loudly proclaimed that they would maintain the collective farms. They approved, so they said, of the superior methods of agriculture which collectivization made possible. But Alfred Rosenberg, the world's most vitriolic anti-Semite and most brutal anti-Slav, has been sent by Hitler to rule the occupied parts of Russia, and he has been outlawing the collectives. He is breaking them up into individual farms. He never would have done it had Germany been in a position to provide the collectives with machinery and to find enough trustworthy Russians to supervise the proper operation of such agricultural enterprises. But neither Rosenberg nor his assistants are trusting the Russians with the management of any farms. In Holland, in Belgium, in Denmark, and in Norway Nazi agents are seeking to round up experienced agriculturists to go to Russia and direct the work on these individual farms. Among all the millions of Russians in the conquered parts of Russia, the Nazis have been unable to find an appreciable number of natives who would execute Nazi orders or whom Nazis could and would trust with their orders!

If Hitler has failed to establish a Vichyite government in a part of Russia that is much larger than France and more populous and that includes such cities as Kiev, Smolensk, Kharkov, Minsk, and Simferopol, what reason is there to believe that he would be more successful if he occupied even more Russian territory and held the cities of Moscow, Leningrad, Kazan, Saratov, Kuibishev? Moreover, if the Russians were thinking of placating Hitler or entering into an agreement with him at the expense of the Allies, would they have been scorching the earth as brutally as they have been doing? Would they have blown up the leading streets in Kiev, their most beautiful and most ancient city, sacred alike to Russian and Ukrainian as the cradle of their nationhood? Would they have dismantled factories and blown them to dust? Would they have burned wheat fields or applied the torch to grain elevators? What other conquered nation or conquered part of the world—including, of course, Malaya, Singapore, the Dutch East Indies—has before its fall dynamited and turned to cinders farms and factories, cities and villages on a scale even remotely comparable to that of Russia, and often enough in complete disregard of the fate of the people who were left behind?

Nor must we imagine that the Russians are not thinking of their future. I doubt if any other nation which is fighting the present war is thinking more earnestly of the future than is Russia. Since the coming of the Soviets Moscow has been haunted by the dread of "capitalist encirclement" and of an all-out war with capitalist enemies.

The ruthlessness of the dictatorship and the decisiveness with which it disregarded and depressed the standard of living and the liberties of the people for the sake of building up an industry and a military machine, were in large measure the outcome of this dread. Since Germany and Japan have become *the* enemy nations, Moscow would welcome nothing more than so to weaken and cripple them as to make it impossible for them ever again—or at least for a long time to come—to put themselves in a position to threaten or to wage war. Therefore, for Russia to favor either Germany or Japan, directly and indirectly, would only serve to frustrate this aim and would rebound to her own immediate and eventual disadvantage.

Nor would the Russians be so inhuman and unselfish as to forgive Germany the ruin and depredation she has visited on an area three times the size of the Reich and on at least ten million Russian families. It is not in the nature of the Kremlin ever to forgive opposition or damage to its own domain. With all the vigor at its command the Kremlin would seek reparations, would demand from Germany compensation for the devastation she has wrought on the Russian land and on Russian humanity. But a separate commitment with Germany, while the Kremlin still possessed fighting strength, merely for the purpose of hurting or crippling capitalist allies, would make the collection of such reparations at least uncertain and might only invite catastrophe. For this reason alone, unless Russia is completely vanquished, which I cannot imagine, all talk outside of Russia, particularly in America, of a separate peace between Moscow and the Fascist powers in Europe and in Asia, is lacking in sense and in logic. Even if we assume that Russia is secretly plotting to betray and ruin her allies, she most certainly cannot be plotting her own betrayal and her own ruin. Lack of trust in her allies most certainly exists, just as a lack of trust in her by her allies is not lacking. But that is something else and offers no ground for the assumption that merely to hurt her allies because they are capitalist, Russia will aid the Fascist power and thereby alone hurt herself perhaps even more than her allies.

Yet by all manner of intrigue Hitler will seek to break up the alliance of the United Nations, particularly between Russia and the English-speaking peoples. He needs nothing so desperately as peace so that he can consolidate his gains and make ready for further conquests. If he attains any more successes over the Red armies, he will seek to pit Russia against the English-speaking nations and the latter against Russia. Nothing would please him more than to conclude peace with Great Britain and America at Russia's and even at Japan's expense. He will have plausible enough arguments to offer to the English-speaking peoples. He will point to Russia as their enemy as well as his. He will not hesitate to single out Japan likewise as a common foe. He will brandish before them with far more gusto than the Kaiser ever could the "yellow peril" of a conquering Japan. He may even stage a "Bolshevik" revolution in one of the conquered countries such as Poland, Slovakia, Hungary, Rumania, for the sake of frightening the business and propertied groups in the English-speaking world into a favorable consideration of his peace offer.

Simultaneously he will feel out Russia for a peace at the expense of the British Empire and the United States and other members of the United Nations. He will offer Russia territorial compensations elsewhere if only he be allowed to keep the Ukraine and other parts of European Russia. In approaching Russia, he will pose as the enemy of capitalism and, therefore, as the man who has much in common with Bolshevism, just as in approaching the English-speaking peoples he will pose as the defender of capitalism and the foe of Bolshevism. He has done it before, with no little success; he will do it again. He will press his intrigue with cajolery, with promise, with threat, with every other conceivable weapon. He will stop at nothing to achieve his end which is peace, especially if, despite victories in the battlefield, he should come to realize the hopelessness of Germany's position because of shortages of oil or some other circumstance. It does not seem possible that in the light of the man's past record he will succeed in any further intrigue either with the Russians or with the English-speaking peoples. But then—it is no use being categorical on the subject.

Yet a separate peace at one or the other's expense will neither destroy nor mollify the irreconcilable antagonisms between Sovietism and Nazism, or Russia and Germany. The Soviet idea and the Nazi idea are mortal enemies, and so are an imperialist Germany and a Russia that will not be swallowed by such a Germany. For Russia this is a battle unto death, and the Russia of today is equipped for such a battle as no Russia ever has been in all history. No other Russian government has had the industries and the agriculture that the Soviets have, or such complete control of both. Nor have the people ever been more firmly united. Soviet Russia knows as old Russia never did how to organize large-scale industry and large-scale agriculture. Cost does not dismay the present-day leaders—either in substance or in blood. Above all, Soviet Russia has learned how to organize armies and how to fight modern wars. No one has learned it any better, no one in the world! With these newly uncovered gifts and talents and imbued with its own idea of civilization, this Russia can go on fighting from the Urals, from central Siberia, from Central Asia, from the Arctic lands, fighting to the bitter end.

This Russia knows only too well that to capitulate to Hitler is to invite tortuous strangulation of nationhood, of culture, of Sovietism, and of the very lives of millions; indeed, is to bring on a fate more horrifying than was the Mongol invasion in the thirteenth century.

This Russia can only fight on against Germany as well as against a Japan whose armies may be occupying Russian lands. The Far East as well as Siberia is especially well suited to guerrilla fighting, and even more than during 1918–22, when Japan held all of eastern Siberia, is Russia prepared for such warfare. Nor will Russia be alone in the war on Japan. Whatever may happen in

Europe, Japan can neither suppress nor destroy the re-surgent nationalism of the Asiatic peoples. Russia will work hand in hand with this nationalism if only as a weapon of warfare against Japan. None of the Asiatic nations may care to copy Russia's economic system; they may well fight against any efforts to impose it on them. Chiang Kai-shek's break with Chinese and Russian Communists in 1927 is too recent not to be full of import for Moscow as well as for China. But Russia's Five-Year Plans, especially now when the results are showing themselves in the fighting powers of the Russian armies and the Russian guerrillas, cannot but stir the imagination of the peoples on the mainland of Asia, and particularly of China and India. Already there are voices in both countries counseling the serious study of such plans and their possible adoption, with a view to achieving industrial and military self-sufficiency with native resources and within a short space of time.

If Japan continues to make conquests in Asia, Russian engineers, Russian industrial experts, Russian generals will be at the disposal of Asia's subjected nations and may be expected to wander up and down their far-flung territories and help to build their fighting powers. For Russia it is as important to shatter Japan's military machine in Asia as it is to shatter the German military machine in Europe. If she is driven by Japanese armies inland into Siberia she will unite in every way she can with other Asiatic nations for the final showdown with Japanese militarism.